IT'S ALL RELATIVE

Einstein's Theory of Relativity

It's All Relative

Einstein's Theory of Relativity

by Necia H. Apfel

Diagrams by Yukio Kondo

Lothrop, Lee & Shepard Books
New York

Text and diagrams checked for accuracy by Dr. Lloyd Motz, Professor Emeritus, Department of Astronomy, Columbia University.

 Inquiries should be addressed to Lothrop, Lee & Shepard Books, a division of William Morrow & Company, Inc., 105 Madison Avenue, New York, New York 10016.
Printed in the United States of America.

5 6 7 8 9 10

Library of Congress Cataloging in Publication Data

Apfel, Necia H
It's all relative.

Includes index.
SUMMARY: Discusses the basic principles of relativity and uses "thought experiments" to explain concepts such as the relationship between space and time, gravitation and acceleration, and the curvature of space.
1. Relativity (Physics)—Juvenile literature. [1. Relativity (Physics)] I. Title.
QC173.575.A63 530.1'1 80-28188
ISBN 0-688-41981-X ISBN 0-688-51981-4 (lib. bdg.)

For my closest relatives—
Don, Mimi, and Steve

CONTENTS

Preface

AT THE END of the nineteenth century, many scientists were convinced that we had learned as much as we could about the nature of the universe. How wrong they were! It is hard to imagine such an attitude today. We are living during a period of great scientific inquiry. Many fields of science are on the brink of great discoveries and advances, the future of which cannot be foreseen. Exciting adventures lie ahead.

Much of our current attitude about science and about the universe has been a result of Albert Einstein's theory of relativity. It has given us an entirely new way of looking at the world. Although three quarters of a century have passed since Einstein first began to present his theory, it is still considered by many to be new and revolutionary. Experiments are still being devised to prove its many predictions.

A knowledge of advanced physics and math is necessary to comprehend Einstein's theory fully, but even without such a background it is possible to understand its basic principles and its effect upon the world of science. We are led into a world at times very contrary to what we experience through our senses. Our "common sense" rebels against what experiment after experiment proves to be true.

Perhaps if such concepts were introduced earlier in our education, they would not be so difficult to accept. The roundness of the earth or its rotation are also not "common sense" conclusions, but we do not question their validity. Our first- or second-grade teacher introduces these basic facts to us and they remain, usually unquestioned, as part of our educational experience.

For this reason, it is important to be introduced to at least a description of the basic principles of relativity as early as they can be understood. Such knowledge should be an integral part of every individual's education. It represents the physics of today and the physics of tomorrow. And, even if you do not choose to enter a scientific field, it will eventually have a profound effect upon your life and your way of looking at the world around you. This book will help prepare you for these changes.

I wish to express my appreciation and thanks to Dr. J. Allen Hynek, Professor Emeritus, Department of Astronomy, Northwestern University, who read the original manuscript and made valuable suggestions and criticisms.

I also wish to thank Nancy Mack, editor of *Odyssey* magazine, for her encouragement in this project.

Lastly, I am most grateful to my husband, Don, for reading the manuscript and offering his suggestions. I also wish to thank him for his patience and love during all the months of writing and rewriting.

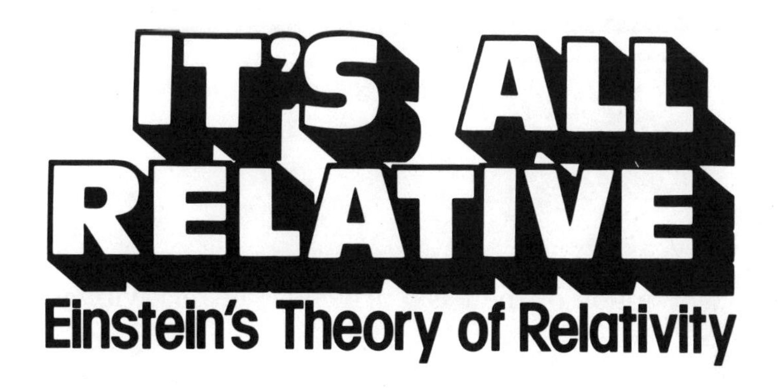

Einstein's Theory of Relativity

Courtesy of the Archives, California Institute of Technology

Albert Einstein in California, 1932.

With the Speed of Light

AT THE BEGINNING of the twentieth century, a young man put forth a theory which has completely revolutionized science. The man was Albert Einstein and his theory was "relativity."

Some of the ideas upon which the theory of relativity is based may seem very strange. Others are very common everyday experiences, but you may never have regarded them as being "relativistic." However, whether strange or not, one by one all of these concepts and assumptions have been or are being proved true and are replacing theories that are hundreds of years old.

To understand the theory of relativity, we must first start with light. Whether it is the light from the lamp or the sun or the fire in the fireplace, there are questions we must ask. How does that light get from there to us? How fast does it go? What is light?

Hundreds of years ago, scientists argued heatedly as to whether light did in fact take time to travel across a space. Some were convinced that light was instantaneously present. It certainly appears to be that way here on earth. We switch on a lamp and the light seems to fill the room immediately. It may have taken 1/200,000,000 of a second, but our senses cannot detect so minute a fraction of time.

Long ago, scientists tried to develop experiments which would prove or disprove that light took a specific amount of time to travel over a given distance, but they did not have accurate enough clocks to measure the movement of light across distances available on the earth. They needed much greater distances—greater than the size of the earth itself—to be able to measure the speed of light.

The first successful measurement came at the end of the seventeenth century. Olaus Roemer, a Danish astronomer, used the four major moons of Jupiter to compute the velocity of light. This was not his original intention. He wanted to measure the time each moon took to orbit the planet. Each of the moons of Jupiter has its own orbit and its own period of revolution around the planet. The periods of revolution are constant and do not change.

Roemer timed the periods by measuring when each moon came out from behind Jupiter each time around. Imagine his surprise when he found that when Jupiter was on the same side of the sun as the earth, the light from the emerging moon came to him 1000 seconds earlier than when Jupiter was on the side of the sun opposite the earth. Why was this?

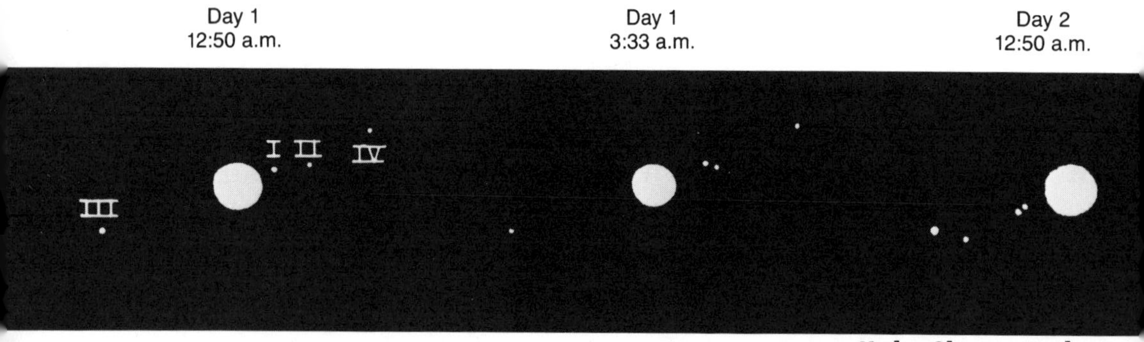

Yerkes Observatory photo

The planet Jupiter and its four largest moons as seen from the earth through a small telescope. Each time one of the moons goes around Jupiter, it passes in front of and then behind the planet.

It was because the light from Jupiter and its moons had to travel much farther when the earth was at point B (on Figure 1) than when it was at point A. This extra distance was twice the distance from the earth to the sun, as you can see on the diagram. By dividing this extra distance by the extra time the light took when the earth was at point B, Roemer was able to

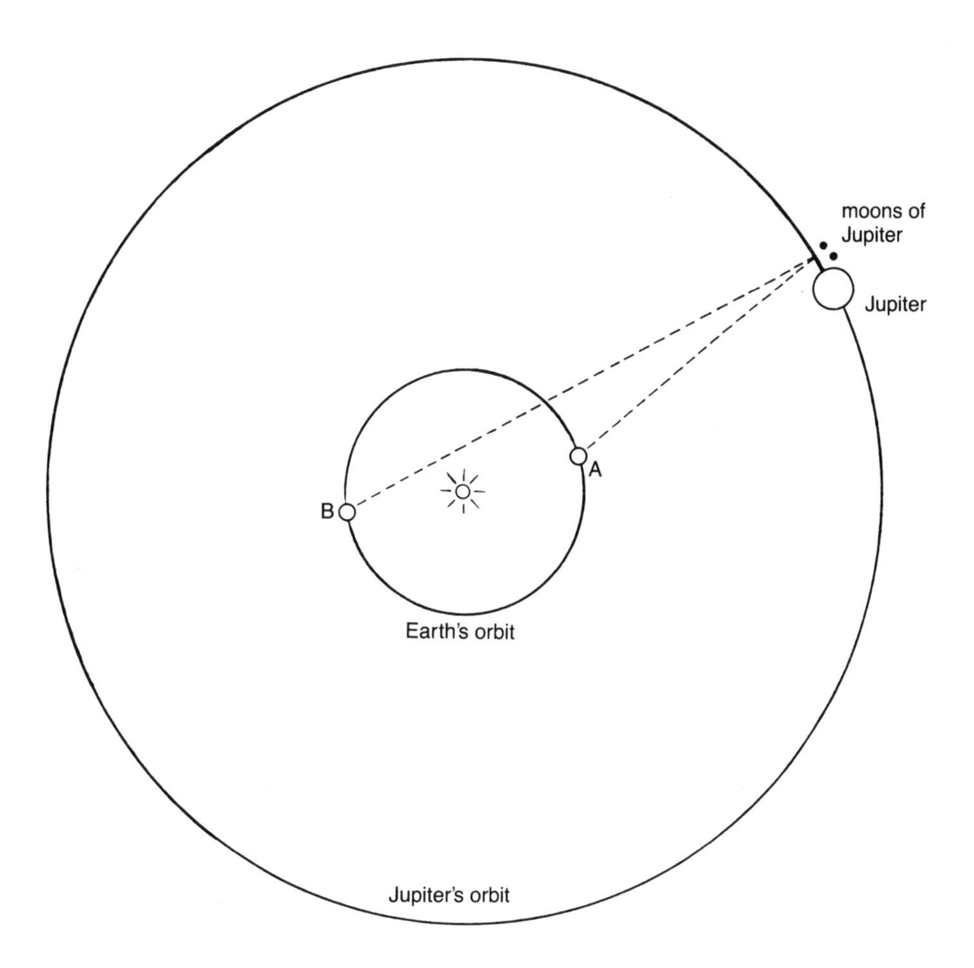

Figure 1. Olaus Roemer's early attempt to compute the velocity of light. Light from Jupiter's moons took longer to reach the earth when the earth was at point B than when it was at point A.

compute the speed of light. He did not have the correct earth–sun distance so his computations were inaccurate, but his method was correct. He finally proved that light does indeed take time to travel across space.

It was not until the nineteenth century that truly accurate measurements of the velocity of light could be made. We now know that light travels approximately 300,000 kilometers (186,000 miles) per second, in a vacuum. (That is about 670 million miles per hour!) This figure has been refined to many decimal places, but for our purposes in learning about relativity the rounded-off value will suffice.

Once it was established that light did indeed take time to travel, the next question raised was, what did it travel through? Sound must have a medium such as air to move through. Sound waves travel through the air or water or other media. These waves hit our ears and cause us to hear the sound. Without a medium to travel through, there are no waves and there is no sound. There is no sound on the moon because there is no air or water. The astronauts had to use radio to communicate with each other when they were in their space suits walking on the moon. (As we will see later, radio waves, like light, do not require any medium to travel through. They can travel through a vacuum at the same speed as light.)

In the nineteenth century, however, it was thought that light was like sound and needed a medium to travel through. Experiments had shown that light, like sound, was wavelike in nature. Therefore it was thought that light, like sound, must travel through something. But it was also known that out beyond the earth in the space between the stars and planets, there is no air or any other matter of much substance. Yet the light from the stars obviously reaches us. It was decided that the "something" that the light must travel through was an "ether." This "ether" was imagined to exist solely for the purpose of carrying light waves. It was supposed to exist everywhere throughout the universe, in the vast emptiness of outer space.

It all sounded very logical. The only problem was that regardless of the method used (and there were many), no one could in any way detect this hypothetical "ether." It remained for a young genius to figure out why this was so. This was Albert Einstein. With his explanation came a completely new way of looking at the universe.

2
What's Relative?

Albert Einstein and his theory of relativity are known throughout the world, although few people truly appreciate the effect this theory has had upon their lives. It has caught the imagination of the general public, but knowledge of advanced mathematics is necessary to understand the complicated formulas that are used to describe it. However, it is possible to discuss its basic ideas and conclusions. It must be remembered that although many parts seem contrary to our common sense, numerous experiments have proved their validity.

Let us return to the nineteenth-century scientists with their hypothetical motionless "ether" which was supposed to be present throughout the entire universe. The scientists reasoned that since the earth was moving through this ether, they should be able to detect and time such motion. They believed that such motion was similar to that of a ship moving through very still waters. They set up their experiments with this concept in mind.

Imagine that you are standing on the outside deck of a rapidly moving ship. The motion of the ship through the water creates a wind blowing in the direction opposite to the one in which the ship is moving. You can feel this wind in your face if you turn toward the front of the ship. It is similar to the breeze that you feel even on a calm, windless day when you ride your bicycle down the street.

On the deck of your imaginary ship, you and your friend are having a game of catch. When you throw the ball toward the front of the ship, the wind, which is blowing into your face, will slow up the ball. When your friend throws the ball back to you, the wind makes it go faster. Of course, if the two of you went below to an indoor room, you could have your game of catch without any such problems.

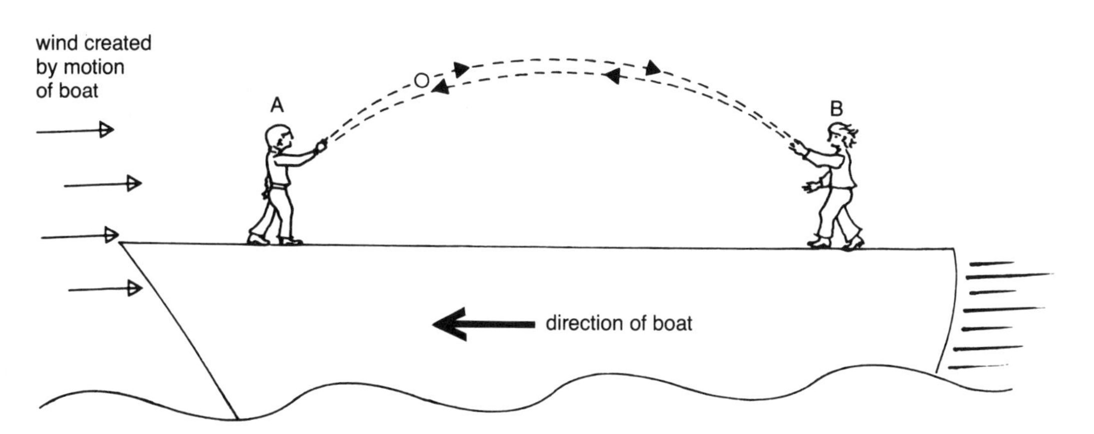

Figure 2. Game of catch: If both players throw the ball equally hard, the ball will travel faster from A to B than from B to A. The wind will affect the velocity of the ball.

The nineteenth-century scientists reasoned that since the earth was supposedly moving through the all-pervasive "ether" in the same way that a ship moves through calm waters, it too would create a wind, an "ether wind" which would affect anything moving through it. Since light was supposed to be carried by this motionless ether, it could be used as their "ball."

A light ray "thrown" or projected in the same direction as the earth was moving would encounter an "ether wind" blowing against it, slowing it up, just as your ball was slowed up in its flight from you to your friend. The ether itself was considered motionless, but the earth's motion would create this "wind." In the same manner, a light ray beamed in the opposite direction to the earth's motion was believed to be aided by the "ether wind" and therefore should move faster.

Using the earth itself as their ship, two American physicists, Albert Michelson and Edward Morley, set up an elaborate experiment in 1881 in an effort to detect these changes in the velocity of light rays as they were "thrown" forward and backward. But unlike the case of the ball's being thrown on the deck of our imaginary ship, there was no detectable change in the velocity of the light rays. And since a change would have confirmed the existence of the ether, this too remain unproved. What was wrong?

Albert Einstein was only twenty-six years old in 1905 when he published an article that not only answered the riddle but also started scientists toward discoveries far beyond anyone's wildest expectations, including those of Einstein himself. His

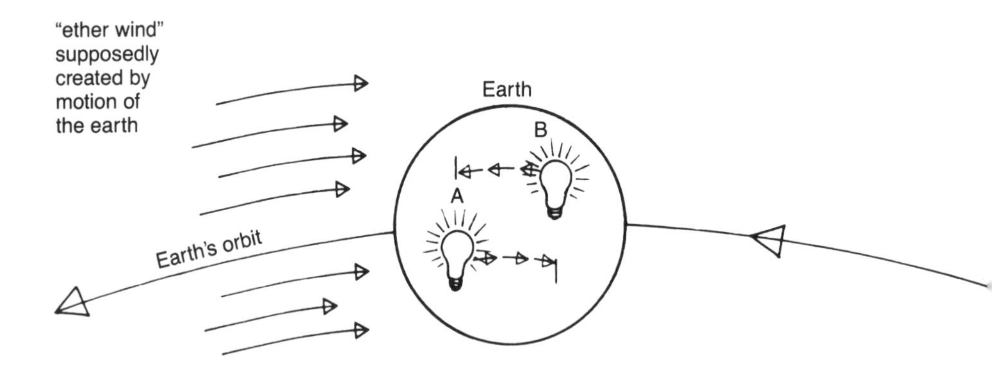

Figure 3. Light from A was thought to travel faster than light from B because of the "ether wind." However, "ether wind" did not affect the velocity of the light regardless of its direction.

Albert Einstein as a young child.

Einstein Archives. Courtesy AIP Niels Bohr Library

first conclusion was that the "ether" was impossible to detect from the earth. Let us see why this is so.

Have you ever been in a train looking out the window when a faster train going in the same direction passed by? Did you have the sensation that you were moving backward even though you knew your train had not changed direction? Relative to the ground, you were moving in one direction—but relative to the other train, you were moving in the opposite direction! Which way were you moving?

It all depends upon your "frame of reference." Were you measuring your velocity relative to the ground (which is the way we usually measure our everyday travel) or were you measuring your velocity relative to the other train? For a few minutes you had switched your frame of reference to the other train and so you were momentarily disoriented. But both velocities can be considered correct within the proper frame of reference.

We cannot speak of the velocity of an object unless we have a frame of reference. In a car we travel 55 miles per hour relative to the ground or the earth. A fly buzzing around inside the car may be flying at only 10 miles per hour relative to the car. An observer along the roadside would say that the car and everything in it was moving at 55 miles per hour. When the fly was flying toward the front of the car, the observer would say that it was flying at 55 + 10 or 65 miles per hour relative to the ground. Meanwhile, the earth is moving in its orbit at 30 kilometers (18 miles) per second relative to the sun. And the sun moves around our galaxy, the Milky Way, at 240 kilometers (150 miles) per second relative to the center of the galaxy. Nothing in the universe can be used as a stationary reference point. Everything is in motion at a velocity that can only be

Figure 4. The driver sees the fly move at 10 mph toward the front of the car. The car is going 55 mph relative to the road and the observer on the sidewalk. The observer therefore sees the fly in the car flying at 65 mph.

measured relative to some other object which is also in motion. We can only detect relative motion.

In order to measure relative motion, we have to be able to detect the reference point past which we are moving. The

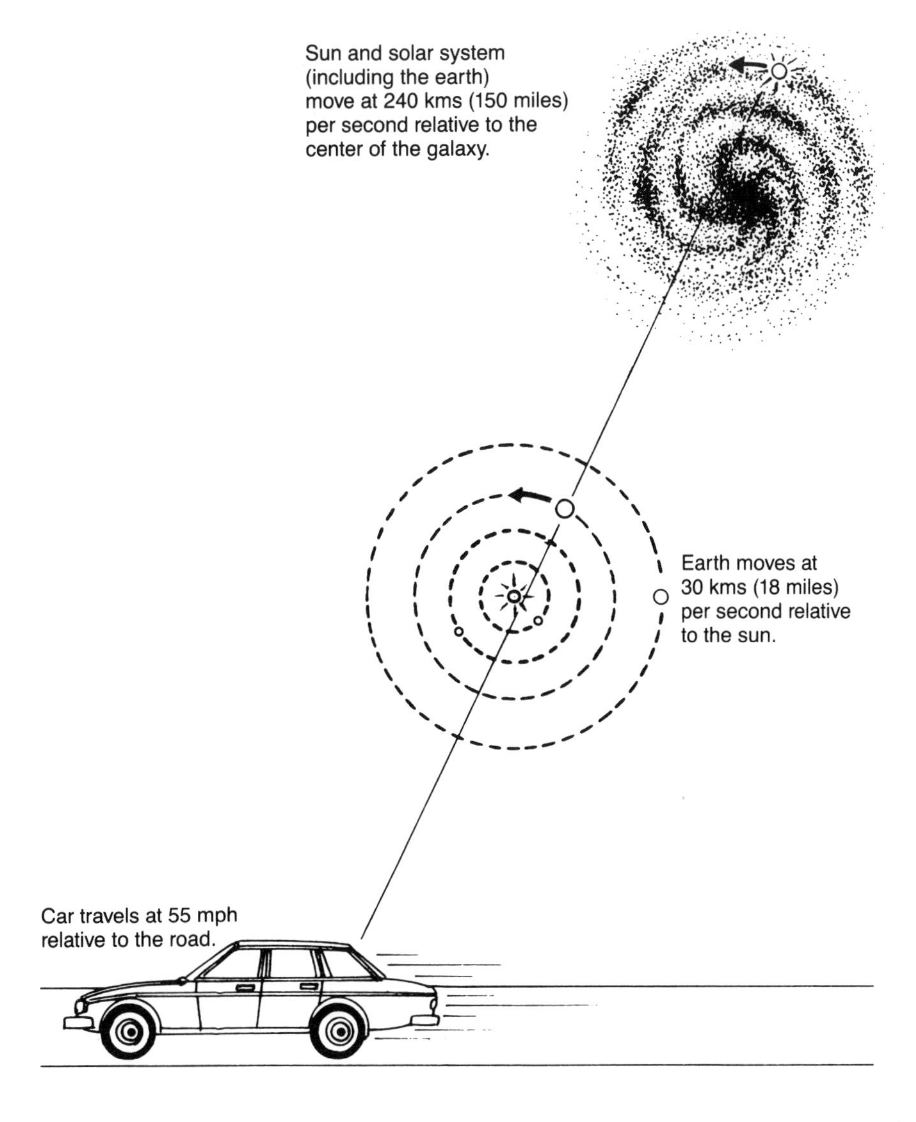

Figure 5. How fast is the car going?

passing train and the ground were reference points in one of our examples. They are moving too, and all we can determine is how fast we are moving relative to their motion. There is no "absolute motion" by which everything else can be measured.

On the train, you could look outside to determine your velocity relative to the desired reference point. But now imagine that you are in an airplane that is flying very smoothly across the country. The shades are pulled down so that you cannot see outside. And you have no access to the instruments in the pilot's cabin. There is no way you can determine how fast you are moving or whether you are moving at all. You will not feel motion if the flight is smooth and at a uniform velocity.

Scientists even before Einstein knew that in such a situation there was no experiment or test that could be performed which would indicate how fast you were going. You must be able to see or in some way detect yourself moving relative to some other object in order to determine your velocity relative to that object. When the scientists attempted to detect the earth's motion through the ether, they were like the passengers in the curtained plane. The velocity of light was their reference point from which they hoped to be able to measure the earth's motion and velocity through the ether and therefore prove the existence of the ether. But because this velocity was not influenced by motion through the ether, they could not prove that the ether existed.

Einstein did not say that the ether was nonexistent. He said that it could not be detected. Furthermore, he found that it was not necessary for his theory. All motion is relative, and therefore something that has no motion relative to anything else (like the ether) cannot be detected. He pushed aside the ether hypothesis as unprovable and turned his attention instead to the study of the velocity of light.

Scientists before him had believed that the velocity of light would vary as conditions changed, just as the velocity of the ball changed as you threw it back and forth on the deck of the ship. That is why the scientists believed they could use the velocity of light to detect the ether. Einstein disagreed. He stated that *the velocity of light is constant everywhere and throughout all time.* Whenever or wherever scientists measure this velocity, they will always get the same answer. It does not matter where the light is coming from or who is measuring its velocity. It never varies.

This may seem like a simple enough statement, but actually, as we have seen, it contradicted a basic assumption upon which much of the science of that day was based. It was known that the velocity of a thrown object increased if the thrower was moving in the same direction as the object, and it decreased if the thrower was moving in the opposite direction. We saw that this was true with the thrown ball on the boat and also with the fly in the moving car.

As another example, if you were about to throw a football, you probably would take a few running steps in the direction you planned to throw it in order to give it greater speed. The velocity of the thrown ball would then be a combination of the speed it would have had if you were standing still plus the speed of your short sprint. Of course, if you throw the ball behind you while running forward, its velocity will be less than it would have been when thrown from a stationary position.

Suppose that instead of throwing a ball, you flashed a light ahead of you as you were running. Would the light then travel faster than if you flashed it while standing still? We would need

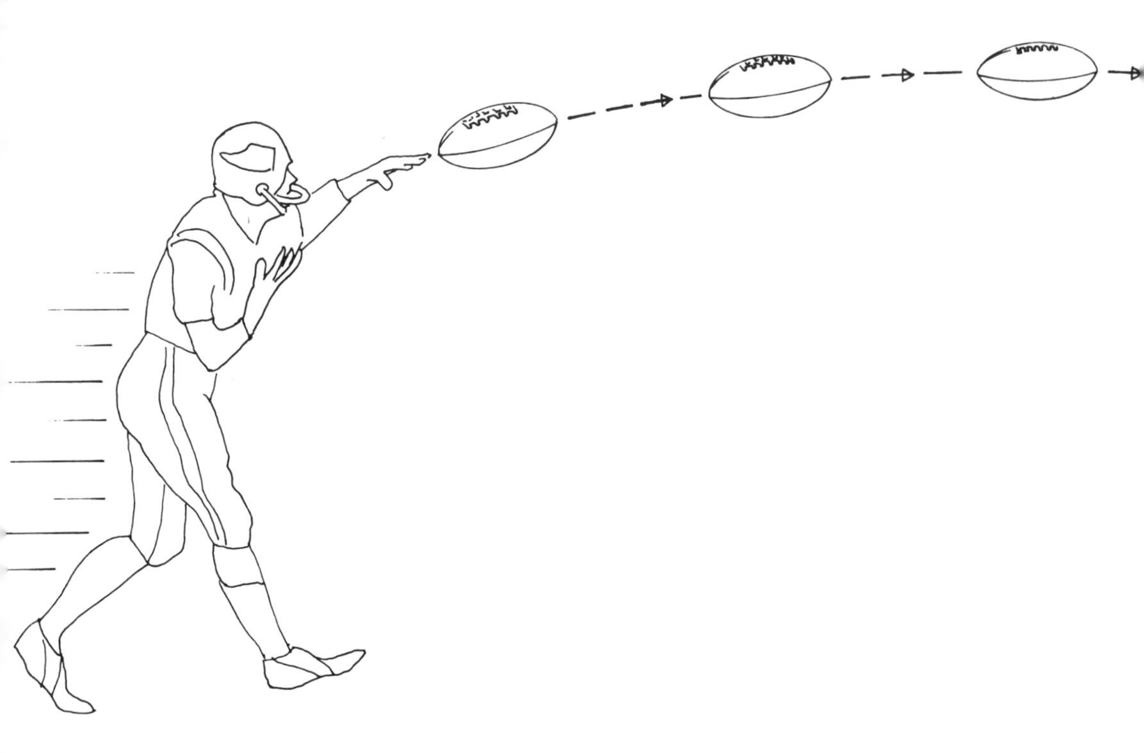

Figure 6. A football moves at the speed it is thrown *plus* the forward speed of the thrower.

an enormous field to test the velocity of light in such an experiment because light travels so very rapidly. Let us instead measure the velocity of light from a distant galaxy. Then the space between the "thrower" (the galaxy) and the "receiver" (the earth) will be great enough to measure the velocity of the "thrown" light.

If the galaxy is not moving relative to the earth, we know that the light will travel at 300,000 kilometers per second. But suppose that the galaxy is coming toward us at, say, 500 kilometers per second. Shouldn't we then measure the velocity of the light to be 300,000 + 500, or 300,500 kilometers per second?

Like the football, the light is "thrown" from a source that is moving in the same direction as the throw. But that is where the similarity stops. According to Einstein's theory, the velocity of light is always the same. We would measure the velocity of the light as being 300,000 kilometers per second regardless of how fast the galaxy was either approaching or receding from us. The velocity or direction of the source of the light or of the observer does not affect the speed of the light. According to the theory of relativity, this is one of the basic laws of the universe. It is here that Einstein differed radically with Isaac Newton and Newtonian science. Let us see what happens when we apply this law to some very fundamental ideas we have about time and space and matter.

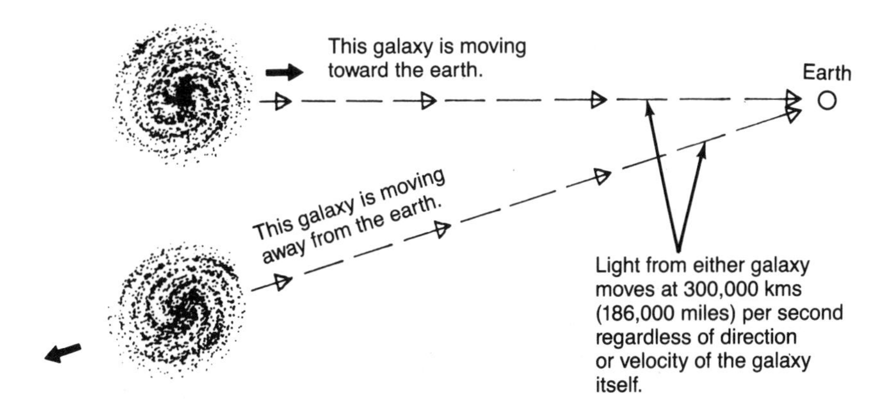

Figure 7. Light from either galaxy moves at 300,000 kilometers (186,000 miles) per second regardless of direction or velocity of the galaxy itself.

3
The Strange and Unexpected

Einstein was fond of using "thought experiments" to help explain his concepts both to himself and to others. By imagining specific situations which would be impossible actually to create, he derived solutions to the problems he was working on. Here is such a "thought experiment."

Imagine that two very large identical spaceships going in opposite directions pass each other very rapidly far out in space. Each ship is moving smoothly with a uniform velocity relative to the other ship. At the very bottom of each ship there is a scientist who is going to measure how long it takes a beam of light to go up to the top of his ship and return. A mirror on the ceiling of each ship will reflect the light beam back down to the scientist. Each scientist has a window at his station so that the other ship can be observed passing by. Each scientist can therefore watch the other scientist at work. Because each ship is moving smoothly, neither scientist feels the motion within his own ship but can see the rapid motion of the other ship as it moves past him. To each one it is the other spaceship that is moving, not his. Each scientist is, in effect, a stationary observer.

Both scientists are going to perform the measurement described above at the same time while the ships are passing each other. Remember that they are far out in space and cannot see the earth or any other reference point. What does Scientist

A see? According to him, the light in his ship goes straight up and comes straight down. He records the time this took to happen. He then looks at B's ship. B is moving very rapidly past him. B's light (according to A) does not go straight up and come straight down. By the time B's light has arrived at the top of his ship, the ship is no longer in the same place. And the same is true of the return trip of the light. Scientist A sees B's light following a zigzag course rather than one that is straight up and down like his own. (See Figure 8.) Both A and B arrive at the same answer for the time that it took their light to travel up to their respective ceilings and come back down again. But A says that B's light traveled a longer route. Both scientists know that the velocity of light is constant and is the same for both of them. Since B has said that the experiment took the same amount of time as A, A concludes that

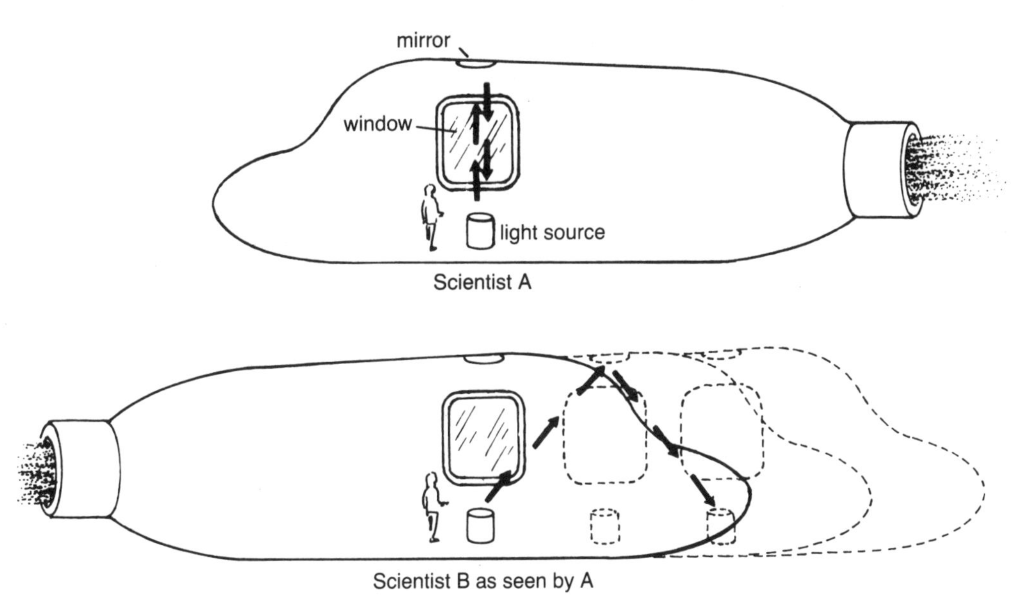

Figure 8. Scientist A sees the light in his ship go straight up and come straight down, but he sees the light in B's ship follow a zigzag course.

B's clock must be running slower to allow the light the extra time to travel a longer distance in the same reported period of time.

Scientist B, looking at A's light and comparing it to the light beam in his own ship, reaches the same conclusion about A's clock. He says that it is A's clock that is running slower since he sees A's light traveling farther than his own. This is called "time dilation," an effect that was predicted by Einstein's theory of relativity. Although both scientists are moving, each considers himself stationary and measures the other ship's velocity relative to this stationary frame of reference. Each will say that the other's time processes seem to have slowed down. Each is correct in terms of his own frame of reference. There is no "correct" clock because the flow or passage of time is a relative quantity. It depends upon the velocity of what is being observed relative to the observer.

Going back to our spaceships, not only do the clocks seem to slow down in the other ship, but everything else seems to go slower also. If our scientists could observe each other for a longer period of time, they would note that the occupants of the other ship seemed to get hungry less quickly, that plants grew more slowly. All time processes are slowed down according to the observers in the other ship. But remember that the occupants of this other ship do not find their own time processes slowing down. Oh no, they say, it is the other ship that has the slower time, not us!

This concept of time dilation is contrary to our daily experiences, as are many other ideas we will encounter in our study of the theory of relativity. We have always considered the passage of time as an absolute quantity. Our "common sense" has told us that it should be the same for everyone and everything. But our "common sense" does not have to deal with velocities approaching the speed of light. To observe even a 10 percent slowing down of the time processes, the ships would have to be moving at one half the speed of light, or about 150,000 kilometers (93,000 miles) per second, relative to each other. At this enormous velocity, the occupants of each ship would note that the other's clock was off by only six minutes for every hour that passed. At nine-tenths the speed of light, the other ship's time processes would be twice as slow as that of the observer. For every hour that passed on the observer's ship then, only one-half hour would seem to pass on the observed ship. It is only at these extremely high velocities that we would notice any relativistic changes.

We cannot test such a theory with actual spaceships, but there are some very tiny subatomic particles called "mu mesons" ("muons" for short) that have proved this concept. When cosmic rays from outer space bombard the air molecules in the earth's upper atmosphere, muons are formed. They plummet down to the earth's surface at close to the speed of light. Scientists have also been able to create muons in the laboratory but in experiments there, the muons are found to last only about two microseconds (a microsecond is one millionth of a second)! After that time elapses, they disintegrate. If the muons that are formed in the upper atmosphere only existed for two microseconds, they would never be able to reach the earth's surface even if they traveled at the speed of light. At best, they would descend about a kilometer (three fifths of a mile). But scientists have found them in great numbers at the surface of the earth, which is about 30 kilometers (18 miles) from where they were formed. They have moved relative to the earth at speeds very close to that of light, and therefore their time processes (by our clocks) have slowed up. They actually disintegrate in two microseconds by their "clocks," but by our clocks their existence is stretched up to fifty times longer. For this reason, they exist for a longer period of time when measured by our clocks and are therefore able to travel a much greater distance before breaking up. That is why they are found on the surface of the earth.

If time dilation affects the existence of subatomic particles, theoretically it can also affect human life. Let us imagine that an astronaut is ready to take off from the earth for an extensive journey in space. His spaceship is capable of reaching velocities extremely close to that of light so that, by earth standards, it will take him about sixteen or seventeen years to reach the bright star Sirius and return to the earth.

He will return to the earth at the expected time sixteen years later, but as far as he is concerned only one day or so will have passed. Everyone else on earth will have aged sixteen years, but our astronaut will have aged only one day. His clocks and other time processes will have slowed down by earth standards during the journey, but as far as he is concerned time will have passed very normally. He will have eaten only a few meals and have shaved perhaps once, while his friends will have dined and shaved many thousands of times. His heartbeat and his breathing rate will also have slowed down by earth's time, although if he had timed either by the second hand on his wristwatch during the journey, he would have found both quite normal. Can this really happen? According to the theory of relativity, it most certainly can! Just as with the muons, because the astronaut was moving at speeds close to that of light relative to the earth, he aged more slowly and could live longer by terrestrial time.

Let us return to our traveling spacecraft. Another strange effect of their relative motion is that each would see the other as having shrunk in length. This would be true for the entire ship. Passing each other at half the speed of light, each 200-foot spaceship would appear to the other ship to be only 170 feet long. At nine-tenths the speed of light it would appear to shrink still further, to only 100 feet. Neither ship, of course, would feel this apparent contraction in its own size any more than it felt any time dilation. And neither would see any change in the width or height of the other ship, but only in the length that is in the direction the two craft are moving relative to each other.

Although the observed ship would seem shorter in length, it would actually increase in mass. We measure mass on the earth by the weight of an object. A Ping-Pong ball is about the same size as a golf ball, but their weight is quite different. The golf ball has a greater mass. There are more and heavier molecules of matter in it.

Going back to the spaceships, when they are moving at nine-tenths the velocity of light relative to each other, each will measure the other as having twice the mass that it has. If the two ships should collide, that extra mass would be a factor in the destruction that would take place. Each would feel that it had been hit by an object with double its own mass.

Once again, we cannot send spacecraft out into space to test these ideas, but we can find verification at the subatomic level. In laboratory synchrotrons, electrons and other charged subatomic particles can be accelerated to very close to the speed of light. Strong magnetic fields are used to keep the particles moving in circular paths. When such experiments were first started, it was found that the magnetic fields had to be made up to two thousand times stronger than had been anticipated by pre-relativity mathematical calculations. The mass of the rapidly moving electrons had increased two thousand times from their normal amount, and therefore the magnetic field had to be extra strong to keep them under control. Since those early tests, subatomic particles have been accelerated much

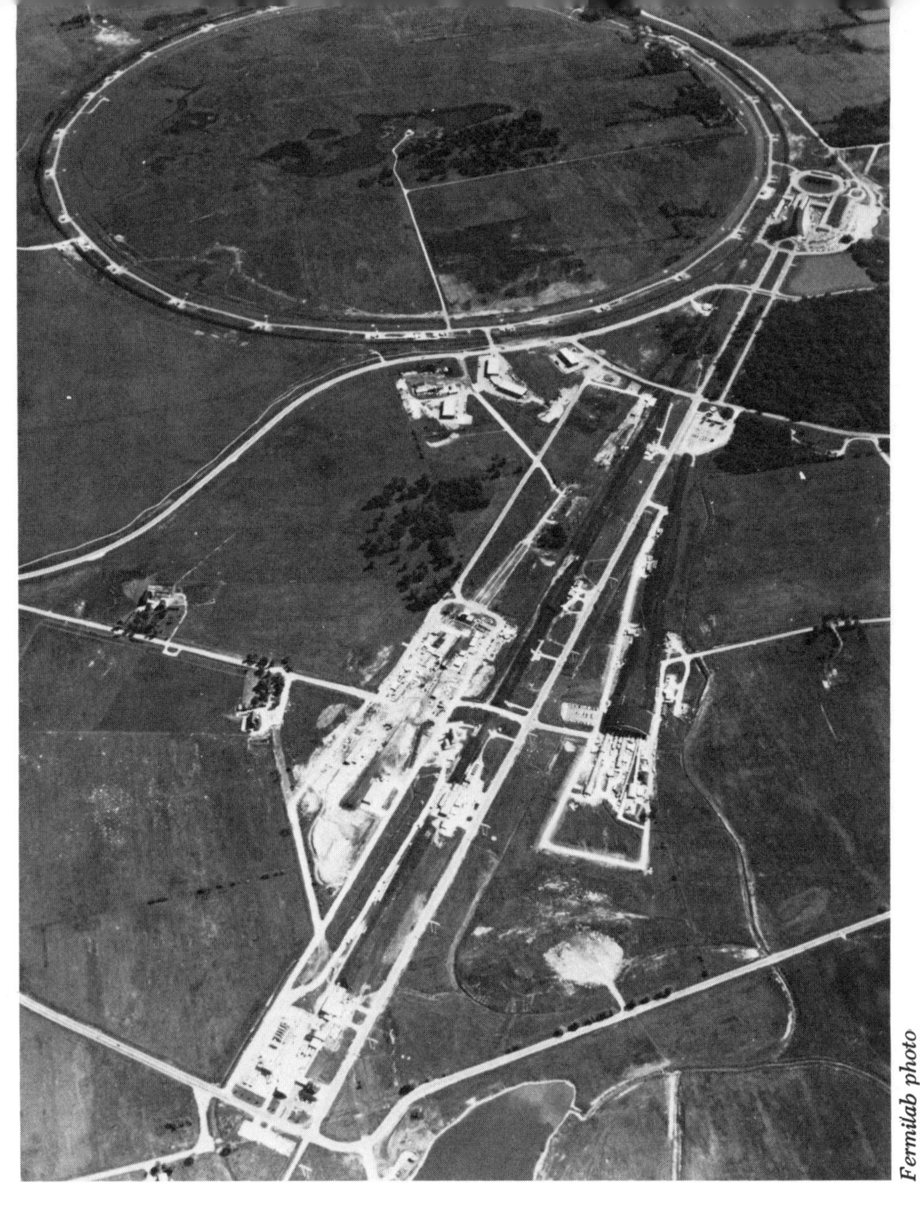

Fermilab photo

Synchrotron at Fermi National Accelerator Laboratory. The circular accelerator ring seen at the top of the photo has a circumference of 4 miles. Hydrogen nuclei (protons) race around the ring about 50,000 times per second with energies up to 500 billion electron volts. Powerful magnets within the ring guide and focus the protons along a very narrow orbital path. Once the desired energy level is reached, the protons are extracted from the ring and transported to other parts of the laboratory.

Fermilab photo

An inside view of the main accelerator at Fermilab. The upper, box-like structure contains the original ring of magnets. The accelerated protons race through a 2″ × 5″ vacuum chamber built into the center of these magnets. The lower structure houses a new proton synchrotron which, when completed, will be capable of reaching one trillion electron volts.

faster. For every increase in velocity, the magnetic field had to have additional strength to handle the ever increasing mass of the particles.

Because the mass of an object increases as its velocity increases, it becomes harder and harder to make the object go still faster. It takes more energy to produce a faster speed. If you had two boxes of the same size and filled one with feathers and the other with bricks, which could you move the faster?

The feathers, of course, assuming that you used the same amount of energy for both. If you could accelerate the box of feathers so fast that it became as massive as the bricks, you would then need the same amount of extra energy to make either box go any faster. The closer either box came to moving at the speed of light, the more massive and heavier it would become. Each increase in velocity would bring an increase in mass, requiring additional energy to make an additional increase in velocity. Eventually the mass would be so great that any effort to move it faster would require more energy than was available—even if you could use all the energy in the universe! And still, according to the formulas of the theory of relativity, your boxes would not yet be traveling at the speed of light. That is why no material object can ever travel as fast as light.

If that is so, what happens when we add the velocities of two spaceships, each of which is traveling more than half the speed of light? If two cars going in opposite directions pass each other on the road and each is going 55 miles per hour, we know that they are moving past each other at 110 miles per hour. We simply add the velocities of the two cars. (Remember that the 55 miles per hour is measured relative to the ground.) Let us put a third observer out in space with our two spaceships. This observer sees each of the two ships pass by at 100,000 miles per second going in opposite directions. Will the two ships then clock each other's velocity at 200,000 miles per second relative to themselves? No, that would be impossible because 200,000 miles per second is greater than the speed of light. Each ship would clock the other's velocity at only 155 miles per second or about nine-tenths the speed of light.

As with other relativistic effects caused by velocities close to the speed of light, we cannot set up such situations. But there

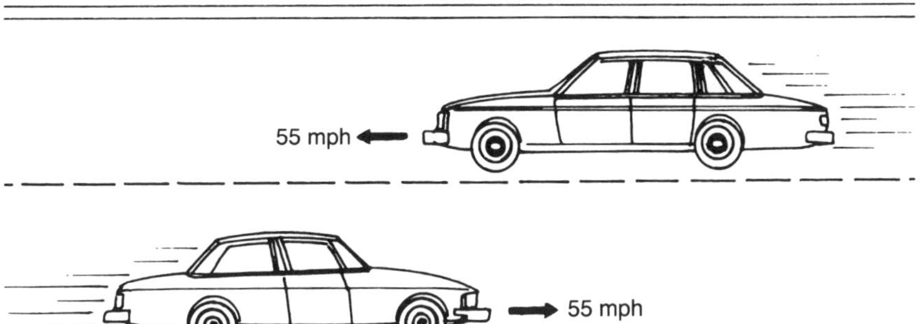

Figure 9. Each car is traveling at 55 mph relative to the observer and the road. They are traveling at 110 mph relative to each other.

are formulas given by the theory of relativity which tell us what these effects would be.

We only have to use the relativistic formula when we are handling velocities that are close to the speed of light. For everyday use, the simple addition formula is sufficient because the cars are moving at such a tiny fraction of the speed of light. To be absolutely accurate, if it should be necessary, we would have to use the relativistic formula to determine the exact velocity of one car relative to the other. But even if our passing cars were each going 100 miles per hour, we would find that their exact relative velocity would be about a millionth of an inch less than 200 miles per hour. That is a good example of why we are not usually aware of the effects of relativity.

The most far-reaching effect of the theory of relativity was

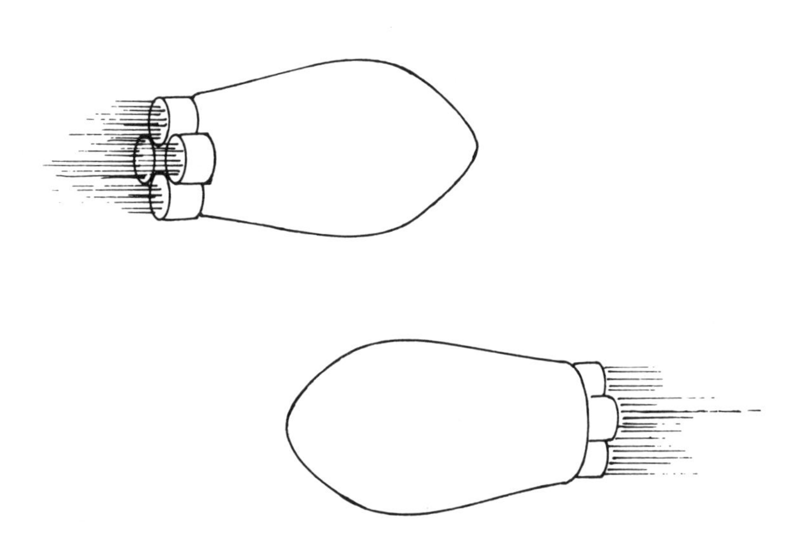

Figure 10. Each spaceship passes the observer far out in space at 100,000 miles per second. However, they are traveling at only 155,000 mlies per second relative to each other.

the development of nuclear energy. The theory stated that a small amount of matter is equal to an enormous amount of energy. The formula for this is: $E = mc^2$. The "m" in the formula is the mass of the object; "E" is the equivalent amount of energy. And "c" is the internationally accepted symbol for the speed of light. Note that the "c" is squared, so even a tiny bit of matter represents an enormous amount of energy. In fact, one gram of matter (about 1/28 of an ounce) is capable of producing about 90 billion kilowatts of power. If we could completely transform one ounce of matter into energy, it would operate more than 2500 automobiles for an entire hour, or it would take one car around the earth about 11,250 times! In synchrotron laboratories, scientists have been able to make this complete transformation at the subatomic level. However, in atomic bombs or in nuclear energy plants, changing the total

The sun, photographed by the Skylab space station astronauts in 1973 while in orbit around the earth. It shows one of the most spectacular solar flares ever recorded, spanning more than 365,000 miles (588,000 kms) across the solar surface.

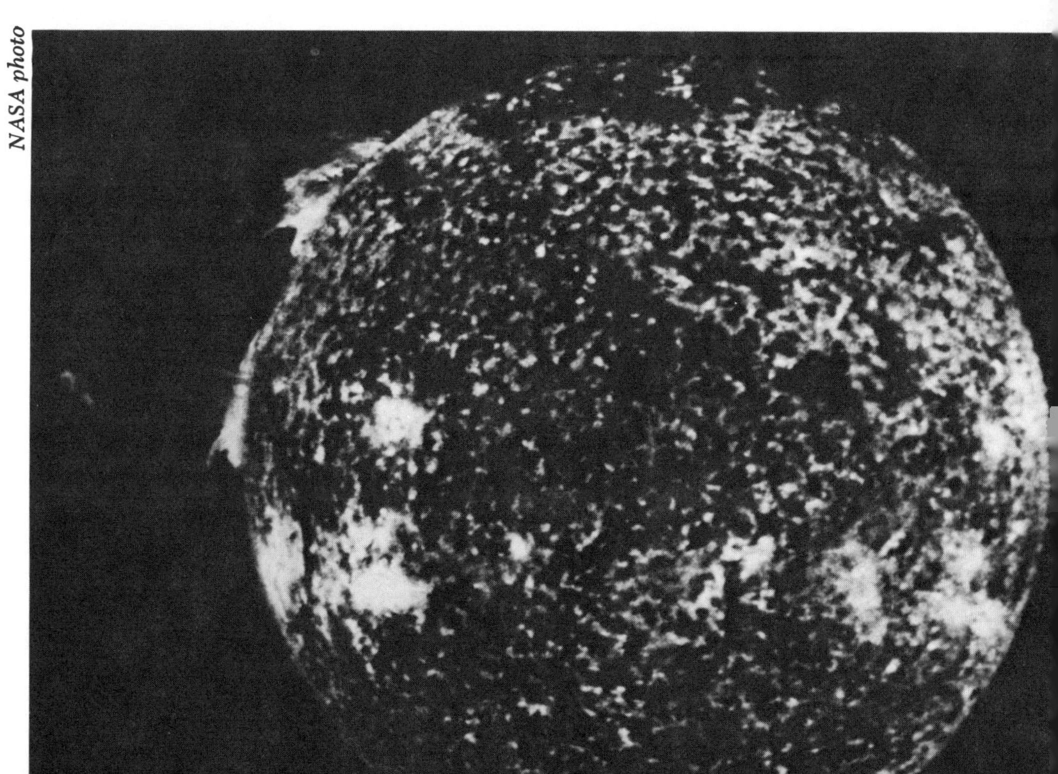

NASA photo

amount of matter to energy has not yet been achieved. But there is no doubt today that the formula is correct.

This conversion of mass into energy is the process by which the sun and all the other stars shine. Over 95 percent of the sun is composed of the elements hydrogen and helium. Deep in the central core, where the temperatures and pressures are enormous, nuclear reactions take place. It is like billions of hydrogen bombs exploding every second. Hydrogen nuclei combine to make helium. It takes four hydrogen nuclei to make one helium nucleus, but in the nuclear process a tiny amount of matter changes into energy. It is this energy which we eventually receive as sunshine and other forms of radiation. If we use Einstein's formula, we find that the sun uses up about four and a half million tons of its mass every second to produce the energy that keeps it shining. This sounds like a tremendous amount, but even in a billion years it will represent only about one percent of the total solar mass.

Albert Einstein's theory of relativity introduced many strange and puzzling concepts. We find that we can no longer trust our powers of observation or our intuitive sense to understand our universe. The assumptions and predictions made by the theory of relativity, most of which have been put into mathematical form, have proved to be correct. The basic foundations of this theory must now be accepted as having been verified.

The Principle of Equivalence

THUS FAR WE have been talking about objects that were moving at uniform velocities. They did not speed up or slow down. Our scientists in their spaceships passed each other at speeds that did not change relative to each other while their observations were taking place. The boat on which you and your friend were playing ball was moving at a steady velocity through the water.

Let us turn our attention now to objects whose velocities do change relative to each other. They accelerate or decelerate while the experiments or observations are taking place. The study of such objects and their non-uniform or varying velocities was the second major part of Einstein's theory of relativity. The first part, which we have discussed, was presented by Einstein in 1905. Subsequently it became known as the "special theory of relativity." The second part of Einstein's theory, which he presented in 1916, was called the "general theory of relativity."

Remember that we are only *describing* the theory and its predictions. Its mathematics are not studied until advanced physics courses in college, which usually include only the equations of the easier special theory. The more advanced general theory equations are taken up at the graduate level.

In order to describe the general theory of relativity, we must first define non-uniform velocity or "acceleration." You feel

Einstein Archives. Courtesy AIP Niels Bohr Library

Albert Einstein in 1916, just after he had completed his theory of relativity.

the effects of acceleration when a car in which you are riding starts moving faster and faster. You are pushed against the back of your seat until the desired velocity is reached and a steady, constant speed is maintained. Then the pressure pushing you back disappears, even though you are now traveling much more rapidly than before.

When the car slows down, you feel a reverse pressure pulling you forward until the "negative acceleration" or "deceleration" stops. As you well know, if the slowing down is very sudden, you may be thrown violently forward and possibly injured.

We usually think of acceleration only as a change in velocity, but in physics the term "acceleration" is also used to describe a change in the direction of a moving object. We experience such an acceleration if our car goes around a sharp curve at a constant speed, that is, without slowing down. We are thrown to one side of the car in the same way that we are thrown forward or backward when the car accelerates or decelerates while moving in a straight line.

When we speak of the velocity of a car in terms of miles per hour, its acceleration power can be expressed as its ability to go from, say, zero mph to 50 mph in ten seconds. Such a car can be said to accelerate 5 mph every second. If it accelerates smoothly, it will reach 5 mph by the end of the first second, 10 mph by the end of the second second, 15 mph by the end of the third second and so forth.

In the same way, if a marble is dropped from a very tall building it will fall faster and faster until it reaches the ground. Its accelerator is the pull of the earth's gravity. By the end of the first second it will be traveling downward at a velocity of 32 feet per second, but it will have fallen a distance of only 16 feet. This is half the distance it would have fallen if it had traveled at 32 feet per second for the entire second. It is an

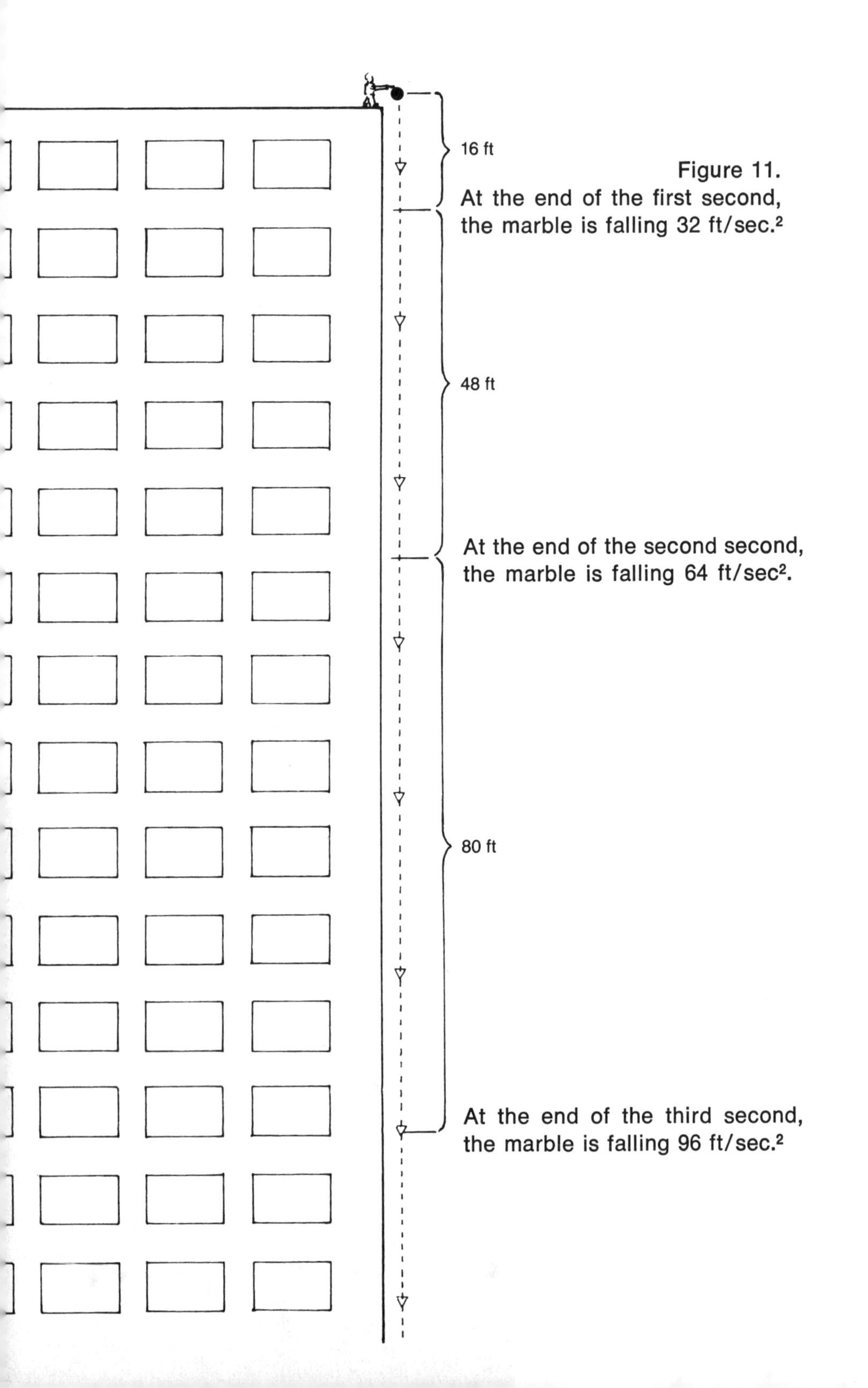

Figure 11.
At the end of the first second, the marble is falling 32 ft/sec.^{2}

average of the beginning velocity (0 ft/sec) and the ending velocity (32 ft/sec).

At the end of the second second, the marble will be dropping at 64 feet per second. Just as it did in the first second, its velocity has increased 32 feet per second. It will drop 48 feet (an average of 32 and 64) during the second second.

At the end of the third second, the marble's velocity will be 96 feet per second, which is another increase of 32 feet per second. It will drop 80 feet during this second (an average of 64 and 96). In the first three seconds of its fall, the marble will drop 16 + 48 + 80 feet, or 144 feet. It has accelerated 32 feet per second every second. We say that its acceleration is 32 feet per second per second. This is usually written 32 ft/sec/sec or 32 ft/sec^2.

If there were no air to slow down a falling body, all falling objects on the earth would accelerate at this rate regardless of their size or mass or composition. The famous scientist Galileo tried to prove this back in the seventeenth century. It is said

AIP Niels Bohr Library

Galileo Galilei (1564–1642). He was the first scientist to use a telescope for astronomical purposes.

that he dropped two balls of different materials from the top of the Leaning Tower of Pisa and they both landed simultaneously. But if he had tried the experiment with a feather and a hammer, the results would not have been the same. The feather would, of course, have floated slowly through the air to the ground rather than falling freely like the hammer.

However, when the astronauts were on the moon (where there is no air), they purposely dropped a heavy tool and a feather from the same height at the same time. Both landed on the surface of the moon simultaneously, dramatically prov-

Astronaut James B. Irwin salutes an American flag planted in the lunar surface during the Apollo 15 mission. The flag was constructed with stiff material so that it would appear to be "flapping in the breeze." There is no air on the moon to create such a breeze.

NASA photo

ing Galileo's theory. The objects on the moon did not fall as fast as they would have on an airless earth, however, because the moon's surface gravity is only one-sixth that of the earth's. This is because the moon is much smaller and less massive than the earth. Nevertheless, both objects fell to the lunar surface with the same acceleration of any free-falling body on the moon.

Now let us try another thought experiment. Imagine that you are in an elevator which is going up in a very tall building. As it accelerates, you feel yourself being pushed downward. If you weigh yourself on a scale while the elevator is accelerating, you will see that you actually are heavier since you are pushing down harder on the scale. A bag of groceries that you are carrying feels heavier, too, because it is also affected.

While the elevator is accelerating, it passes a floor with a glass door so that someone on that floor can see you. At that moment an orange drops out of your bag of groceries and falls to the floor of the elevator. To the observer outside the elevator, the orange will fall at 32 ft/sec^2, the usual free-fall acceleration for objects on the earth. She will see it hit the floor sooner than it would have if the elevator were not moving, but she will realize that that is because the floor is moving upward toward the falling orange and therefore the orange does not have as far to fall.

You, however, are moving rapidly upward at the same speed as the floor of the elevator. To you, the distance the orange falls is not foreshortened by the rising floor. You see the orange fall a greater distance than that measured by the outside observer. However, for both you and the outside observer the orange takes the same time to fall from the bag to the floor. According to your observation, therefore, the orange will fall at a greater acceleration than 32 ft/sec^2. It must do this in

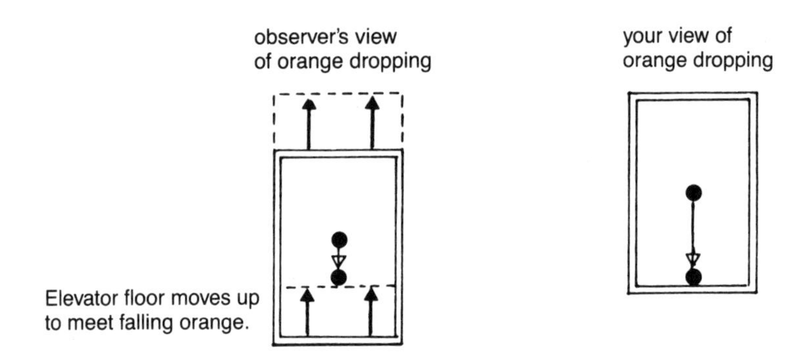

Figure 12. Time interval of falling orange is the same for both you and the outside observer. Therefore the orange, relative to you, must fall faster to cover a greater distance in the same amount of time.

order to cover a greater distance in an equal amount of time. (See Figure 12.)

Let us now imagine that you journey to a planet whose surface gravity is much greater than that of the earth's. You will feel yourself pushed downward toward the floor just as you did in the elevator. You will weigh more on this planet than you did on earth and your bag of groceries will feel heavier also. If an orange drops out of your bag while you are standing on the surface of this planet, it will fall to the ground at an acceleration higher than that of freely falling objects on the earth.

Of course you can tell the difference between being in an elevator on the earth and being on the surface of a faraway planet just by looking around. But if you could not see out of the elevator or you were confined to a small windowless room on the planet, there would be no way for you to distinguish between the effects you would observe and feel in either place. Your weight would be greater than it is when you are standing on the surface of the earth. Objects would feel heavier, too. And freely falling objects such as the orange would accelerate downward at a greater rate than is normal for earth-bound objects. *There is no experiment that you can perform which would indicate whether you were in an accelerating elevator or on a more massive planet.*

It was Einstein who first pointed out that the effects of gravitation and acceleration are the same and cannot be distinguished. They are equivalent, he said, and this fact became known as the "principle of equivalence."

Someday in the future, designers of spaceships may use this principle to create artificial gravity out in space. The spaceship will be shaped like a wheel or a doughnut. When the doughnut-shaped spaceship is rotated, objects and people will be pushed toward the outer rim. This will become their "floor." All their senses will indicate that "down" is in the direction of this outer rim and "up" is toward the center of the spaceship. The occupants will feel as though they were within a gravitational field although in this case it will be caused by a constant

NASA photo

A possible space colony of the twenty-first century. Each of the twin cylinders would be 19 miles (32 kms) long and 4 miles (6400 meters) in diameter. By rotating each cylinder once every 114 seconds, an Earthlike gravity would be created.

change of direction (in a circle) or acceleration rather than by the presence of a massive body like the earth.

Perhaps you have had a similar experience on a carnival ride which rotates very rapidly so that all the passengers are flattened against the outer rim. In this case you can see the amusement park as you spin around, but if you close your eyes you can easily imagine that you are lying on the ground rather than standing upright. The rapid whirling of the wheel has caused you to change your frame of reference for a short period of time.

The principle of equivalence may seem rather obvious now that it has been explained. We have all experienced the heavy feeling that comes from going up in a fast elevator and the lighter feeling when we descend. However, the principle of equivalence had far greater implications for science.

Einstein used the principle of equivalence to develop an entirely new theory of gravitation and an entirely new way of regarding the universe. He rejected Newton's theory of gravitation, which stated that gravitation was a force which emanated from an object and exerted its influence over great distances. The theory that Einstein developed depicts a more accurate representation of the natural laws of the universe. With it, he was able to explain certain phenomena which no one had been able to explain before. So confident was he that the theory was correct that he even suggested three scientific tests which would prove its accuracy. Before we consider these experiments, let us look at our universe as Einstein pictured it in 1916.

5 The Space-time Continuum

Imagine yourself in a railroad train traveling across the flat plains of Kansas or Nebraska. The track is very straight and can be seen stretching out in front of you for miles. At times it may even seem to be endless. Every section of the track looks like every other section, so that to identify any one part of it you would have to refer to some specific landmark nearby. Such a landmark might be a station or a sign or a numbered telephone pole alongside the track. These landmarks or reference points are "coordinates" which locate your train on the track.

The track is an example of a "continuum"—a continuous entity whose parts cannot be distinguished separately without an outside reference point. The train moves in a straight line along this track. It cannot move in any other direction. It must follow the path of the track. In other words, the train can only move in one dimension in space. The track is an example of a "one-dimensional space continuum."

Another example of a continuum is the middle of the Pacific Ocean. It stretches as far as the eye can see. It, too, seems to be endless but not just in one direction like the railroad track. If you were on a ship on the Pacific Ocean, you could move both east or west and north or south. That is, you could move in two dimensions because the surface of the ocean is a two-dimensional space continuum.

Amtrak photo

A train on a straight track moves along a one-dimensional space continuum.

Sitmar Cruises

An ocean liner sails on a two-dimensional ocean surface.

A plane flies in a three-dimensional atmosphere.

United Airlines photo

As with the railroad track, there is nothing on this continuous surface which indicates your position. It all looks the same. Only by looking to some reference points outside the watery continuum can you determine where you are. Sailors long ago used the sun and the stars to help them navigate when land was no longer in sight. Today, sophisticated instruments are used on seagoing vessels, but their readings are still based on the positions of the sun and the stars in the sky. The location of a ship is given in terms of its longitude and latitude, the two coordinates necessary to locate the position of any object on the two-dimensional surface of the earth.

When you travel in an airplane, you can go not only east or west and north or south, but you can also go up or down. The air space in which your airplane moves is three-dimensional. There are no distinguishing landmarks in the air and the space seems to stretch out endlessly. You are flying through a continuum. Of course you can look out of the window and sight landmarks such as rivers or cities on the ground below, but they are reference points outside of the region of space in which you are traveling.

To determine your exact position in this three-dimensional space continuum, you need three coordinates: one to tell you your east-west position, one to tell you how far north or south you are, and one to indicate your height above the ground. The longitude, latitude, and altitude of the airplane pinpoint its location in the earth's atmosphere.

These moving objects—the train, ship, and plane—are not moving in space only. They are also moving in time. Time is passing during their journeys. To describe their motions it is necessary to include a time coordinate along with the space coordinates. For example, the train was at Station A at 2:00; it reached Station B at 3:30 and Station C at 4:00. The times specific events occur (such as when the train reaches a station) become coordinate measurements. To describe the motion of the train along the track, we need two coordinates, one of time and one of space.

The time coordinate is based upon units of time which we can easily measure by outside reference points. The length of our day is measured by the earth's rotation; our year depends upon the earth's revolution around the sun. We have watches and clocks to tell us the hour. We refer to specific events in terms of the time at which they will occur. At 2:00 there will be a history test; at 4:00, a basketball game. The sun will rise at 7:21; spring begins on March 21. These are all time coordinates, by which we distinguish one day or hour from the next. They are all "outside" reference points, just as the train stations were separate from the railroad tracks.

Imagine yourself in a windowless room without any clock or watch. You can neither hear nor see anything outside of this room. The light is kept on day and night and your activities are on no regular schedule. Very soon you will lose all track of how much time has passed. It will all seem the same, day after day. You will not even know whether it is morning or afternoon or day or night. That is because the passage of time, like the railroad track or the ocean surface, is a continuum. It is continuous, without any distinguishable parts. Only by referring to time coordinates which are outside of time itself can we orient ourselves. That is how we "tell time." The time coordinates tell us when something happened just as the space coordinates tell us where it happened.

We usually think of time as being "universal"—that is, the same for everyone at any place. If you witness two events happening at the same time, you assume that everyone else will see them happening that way also. In our everyday activities there is nothing that would lead us to any other conclusion—but we are wrong.

There is no universal or absolute time in the universe. Albert Einstein first pointed this out with one of his famous "thought experiments." As we have seen, these are imaginary situations which would be impossible to create, but which he devised to help clarify his thinking about a problem. Let us, once again, try this method ourselves.

Imagine yourself sitting in a car in front of a railroad crossing waiting for a rapidly passing train to go by. A thunderstorm is in progress and as you wait you witness two strokes of lightning occurring at the same time. You see one far off to the left of your car (A) and the other far off to the right (B).

At the moment that the light rays from the lightning are emitted at points A and B far off to your left and right, a passenger sitting in the train passes directly in front of your waiting car. She is moving rapidly (with the train) toward the beam of light coming from the right (B) and away from the beam of light coming from the left (A).

The two beams of light from the lightning flashes reach you simultaneously, but they reach the train passenger one after the other. She sees B's light before she sees A's. To her the two flashes of light are not simultaneous. Her timing of the two events are quite different from yours. Whose observations are correct?

Both you and the train passenger measured the occurrence of the lightning bolts by when the light actually reached each of you. You are therefore both correct in terms of your own frame of reference. Your frame of reference is the ground or the stationary car, whereas the passenger's frame of reference is the moving train. You do not experience the same events as having happened in the same way. Your timing of the events is different from the passenger's timing because your frame of reference is different. Einstein said that "unless we are told

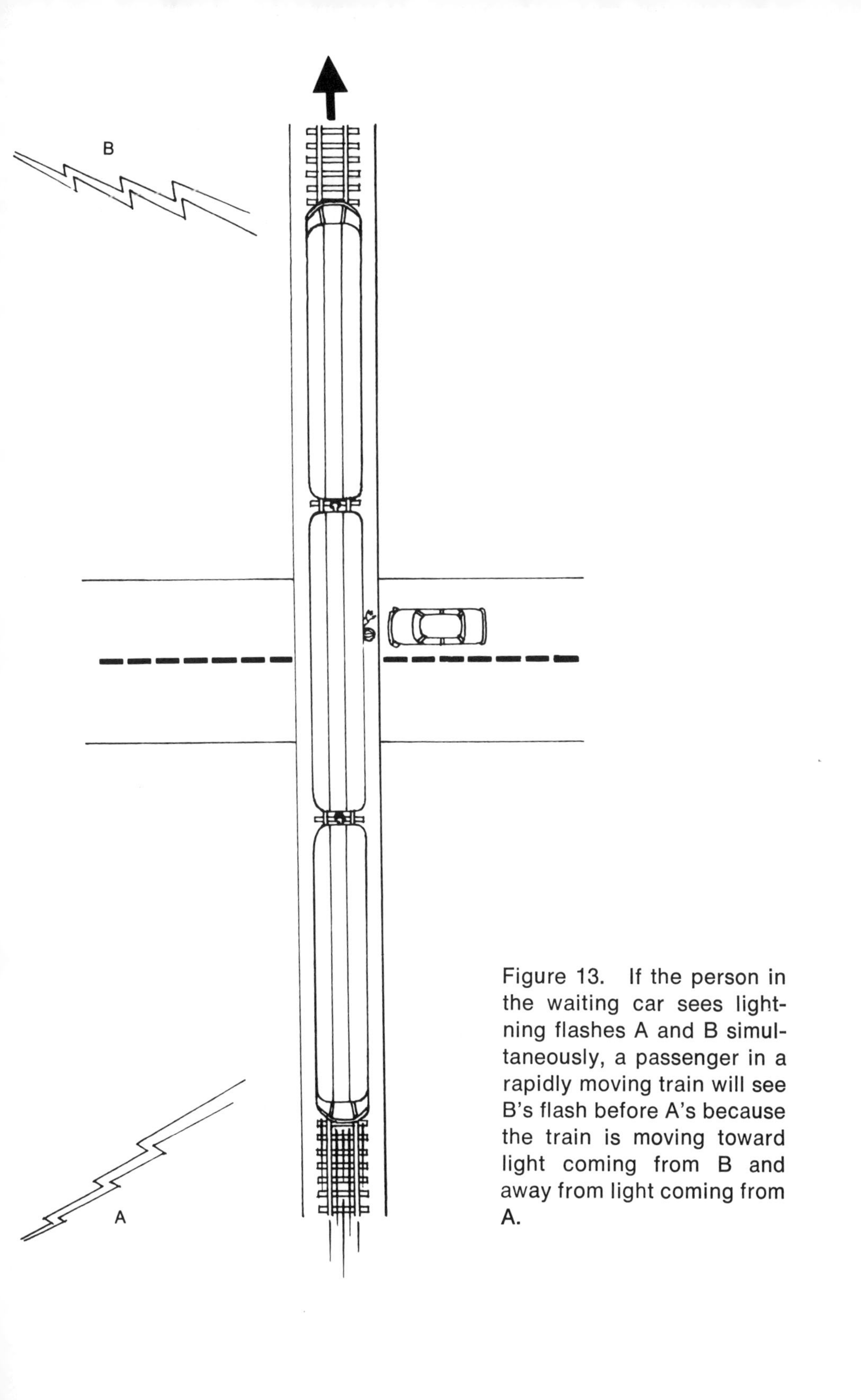

Figure 13. If the person in the waiting car sees lightning flashes A and B simultaneously, a passenger in a rapidly moving train will see B's flash before A's because the train is moving toward light coming from B and away from light coming from A.

the reference-body to which the statement of time refers, there is no meaning in a statement of the time of an event."

With the use of this thought experiment, Einstein showed that words such as "before" or "after" or "past, present, and future" can only be spoken of in terms of a specific frame of reference. This concept is completely contrary to Newtonian theory and also to what our own common sense tells us. Neither Newton nor we ever experienced velocities that even come close to the speed of light. At the speed that even our fastest modes of transportation move, we can never detect any differences between what two observers (you and the train rider) witness when lightning flashes. To stage an actual demonstration of Einstein's thought experiment would require velocities much, much greater than any we encounter in our everyday activities. It took the genius of Albert Einstein to show what would occur in such a situation, even though he, too, could never physically detect it. He presented this thought experiment long before astronomers and physicists realized how important this concept would be to their research.

Let us go back to our railroad train. We can describe its motion along the tracks by the use of a train schedule. It gives the time and the location of each stop along the tracks. The train is actually moving in a *two*-dimensional continuum of *space* and *time. Three* coordinates (latitude, longitude, and the date) are necessary to describe the ocean liner crossing the Pacific Ocean. It moves in a three-dimensional continuum of space and time. The airplane pilot must use *four* coordinates to describe his flight across the country. Three give his location in space and one gives his location in time. He moves in a four-dimensional continuum of space and time.

On the next clear night, look at the stars in the sky. The starlight that you see that night has been traveling through space for many years. It may have taken eight years, eight hundred

Yerkes Observatory photo

A star field.

years or even eight million years or longer for the light from each star to reach you. What you see is a picture of how the stars looked when that light left them, not the way they look today. Each star may no longer look the way it does now. It certainly is not in the same place in space. It may not even exist anymore!

If you should take a photograph of the stars that night, you will then have a permanent record of how the stars appeared sometime in the past. The stars are not all at the same distance from the earth and therefore the length of time it took each star's light to reach you varies greatly. Regardless of how long each star's light has been traveling through space, however, all are recorded on the same photograph. According to our frame of reference here on earth, all the information revealed on that photograph carries the same dateline.

Events on earth	*Stellar objects*	*How many years ago light left stellar objects*
Solar system, including earth, not in existence yet	Quasar OQ 172, most distant object yet detected	15 billion
Microscopic life forming	Quasar 3 C 273	3 billion
Early land plants developing	Cluster of galaxies in Hercules	340 million
First mammals and birds	Cluster of galaxies in Perseus	173 million
First primates	Cluster of galaxies in Virgo	38 million
Earliest man	Andromeda galaxy	2 million
Fall of the Roman Empire, 300–400 A.D.	Orion nebula	1600
Galileo's first telescope, 1609	Pleiades cluster	400
First telephone, 1875	Canopus	98
World War II began, 1939	Arcturus	36
Sputnik launched; beginning of the Space Age, 1957	Vega	23
How old were you 4⅓ years ago?	Alpha Centauri, nearest star to our sun	4⅓

Like the fossils in the ground or the events recorded in history books, the images of stars on a photograph represent many time periods in the past.

When we are gazing at the beautiful starlit sky such considerations are not important. But to the astronomer trying to delve into the mysteries of the universe, such a geocentric (earth-centered) frame of reference is unworkable. The light that our eyes or camera receives is "fossil" light. It is the remains of something that existed in the past. And like the fossils that geologists find in the ground, each star's image on the photograph represents a different time period in the past. The star itself is not a reality until we consider it in terms of time as well as space. We must look at it in terms of "space-time." Then we can place it in its proper location without encountering the dilemma that what is "now" for us is not "now" for the star.

Time and space are thus intimately related. We cannot separate them if we are to depict the real world. No object or person can exist in some location (space) without also existing in some time period. And nothing can exist in time without also existing in space. Although scientists before Einstein were aware of this relationship between space and time, it was Einstein's theory of relativity which showed that there is no separate time or space; there is only "space-time." Our universe is a "four-dimensional space-time continuum." Time is the fourth dimension. We can no more separate the dimension of time from the three dimensions of space than we can separate the width of a house from its depth and height and still show the real picture. All four dimensions are necessary in the real world.

The Theory of Absolutes

No one can visualize a four-dimensional space-time continuum. It is a mathematical concept and can be expressed in mathematical equations, but when we try to put this concept into words, we cannot express exactly what the mathematical ideas convey to the scientist. The equations of the theory of relativity express mathematically the relationship between space and time. It is this relationship that we are trying to define when we speak of time as a "fourth dimension" and when we speak of a four-dimensional space-time continuum.

In Einstein's thought experiment about the lightning flashes, he showed that the recording of events can differ for two observers under certain circumstances. If both you and the train passenger had actually seen the light flashes from the lightning simultaneously, then the two of you would disagree on how far away from the railroad crossing each lightning bolt occurred. Each of you would measure the distance according to your own frame of reference. The amount of difference in the measurements would depend upon how fast the train was moving relative to your stationary car. Whose records can be considered correct? How can the two differing observations be reconciled?

We cannot answer these questions by using only the spatial or temporal dimensions. We must also consider the velocities of the observers relative to each other. Because the observers were not stationary relative to each other, time and space become relative quantities as well. But it is still possible to locate the events accurately in space-time.

In other words, the locations of events in space-time is absolute, not relative. Perhaps a more appropriate name for the theory of relativity would be the "theory of absolutes." In order to see why this is so, first let us look more closely at the concept of a four-dimensional space-time continuum.

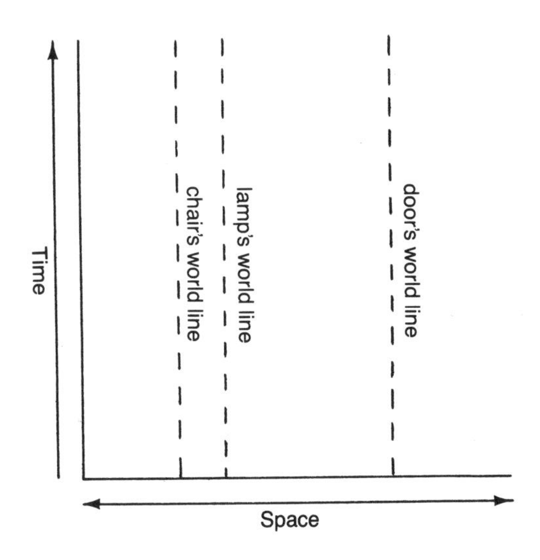

Figure 14. Everything in the universe has a world line.

Right now, as you sit reading this book, you are moving in this continuum. You may not be moving in space but you are definitely moving in time. Everything around you—the chair, the lamp, the floor—is also moving in time. We can draw a diagram of this. We will represent your motion in space along the horizontal axis of our diagram and your motion in time along the vertical axis.

The line representing your motion in space-time is called your "world line." Every particle of matter in the universe has a world line. As you can see in Figure 14, the lamp and the door are also moving in time, but obviously not in space. (Of course, since the door and the lamp are moving with the earth itself, someone not on the earth would draw a different world line for them.)

What happens to your world line if you put down this book and go out to play on a ballfield three blocks away? Note that although you have moved through the three dimensions of space by getting up and walking to the field, the three space dimensions have been combined. This is so that all the motions in space-time can be represented on one diagram.

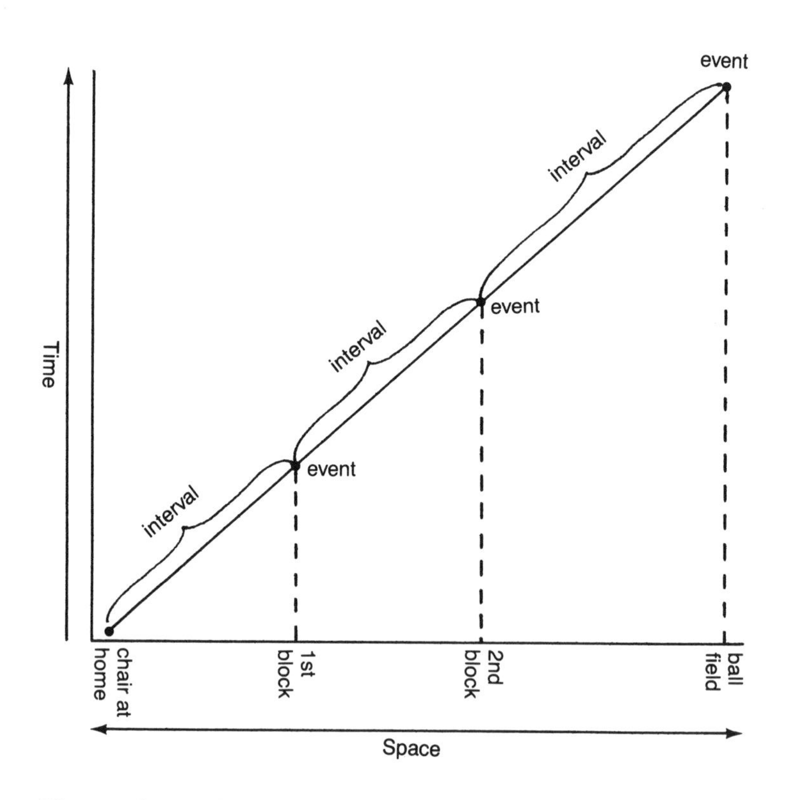

Figure 15. Events and intervals on world lines: a trip to the ballfield.

As you can see, certain places along the route have been marked off on the world line in Figure 15. Your arrival at each of these spots is called an "event" in space-time. Each of the points or dots between each event represents a specific time and location in space-time. The length of the line between any two events is called an "interval." It is the distance between any two events in space-time. We could also break down the world line into smaller intervals by considering, say, each step that you take an event. Because space-time is a continuum, these intervals can be divided into smaller and smaller units, although there is no purpose in doing this in the present situation.

If you stop along the way to the field to talk to a friend, your world line will look like this:

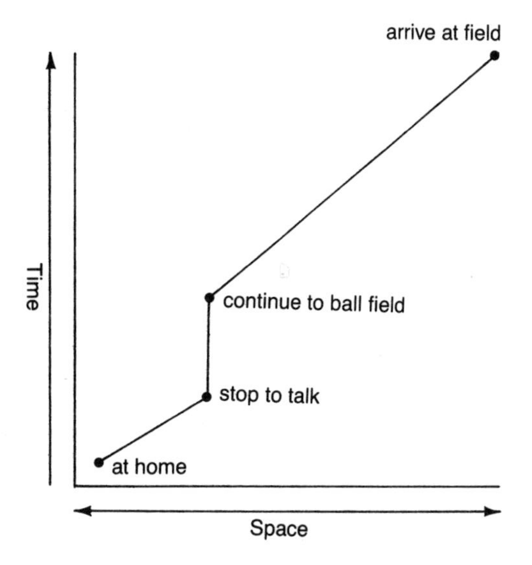

Figure 16. Another trip to the ballfield.

At the point that you meet your friend, your world line "intersects" with his world line. Let us say that he has just come from the field and decides to return to it with you. His world line would intersect with yours as shown in Figure 17.

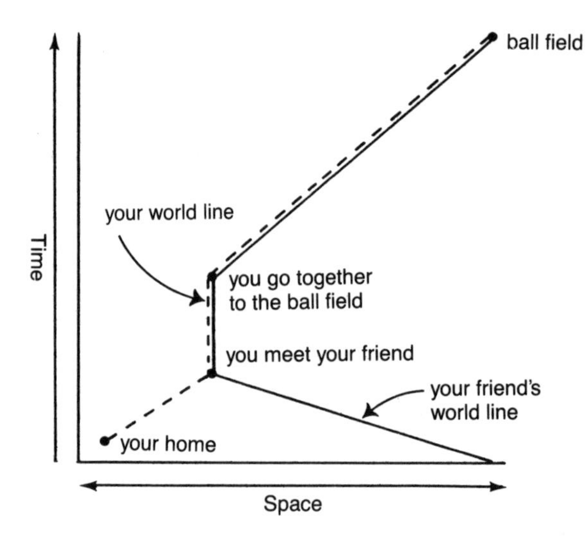

Figure 17. Your world line intersects with your friend's world line.

Your world line is also included in this diagram.

You can probably think of many examples in which the concept of world lines, events, and intervals can be applied. If you expected to get the autograph of a favorite movie star at some shopping center, it would be important that your world lines intersect. Next time you accidentally bump into someone, you could apologize by saying, "Excuse me—our world lines just intersected." You may get a strange look because we do not usually think in terms of world lines in situations such as that. But the concept is basic to the theory of relativity. Let us see why this is so.

According to the theory of relativity, the interval between any two events on a world line is an absolute quantity. It does not matter who is observing the events or measuring the interval. Usually the observer divides the interval into its time and space components and then measures each separately. His or her measurements of each of these components may be quite different from those of another observer in another frame of reference. The measurements of each observer will depend upon his motion relative to the events he is witnessing. But when either observer takes his measurements of time and space and uses them in the equations set forth in the theory of relativity, the space-time interval between the two events will be computed to be the same.

Space-time intervals are the real distances between two events. This distance is measured in both space and time—in space-time. It does not matter who is doing the measuring, where it is being done, or when it is being done; the space-time interval between any two events does not vary. It is an absolute quantity.

Now let us go back to our "lightning flashes" thought experiment in Chapter Five. We saw that the same events were recorded by two observers as having happened at different times because the observers were moving relative to each other. Both measured the time and space components from different frames of reference. However, according to the theory of relativity, the space-time interval between the two events is the same for all observers everywhere.

This is difficult to understand without knowledge of the mathematical computations involved. Once again, let us use an analogy.

The relationship between space and time may be thought of as the relationship between the sides of a "right triangle" in Euclidean or flat (plane) geometry. A right triangle is a triangle that has one "right angle." A right angle is formed when two straight lines are perpendicular to each other. A right angle is

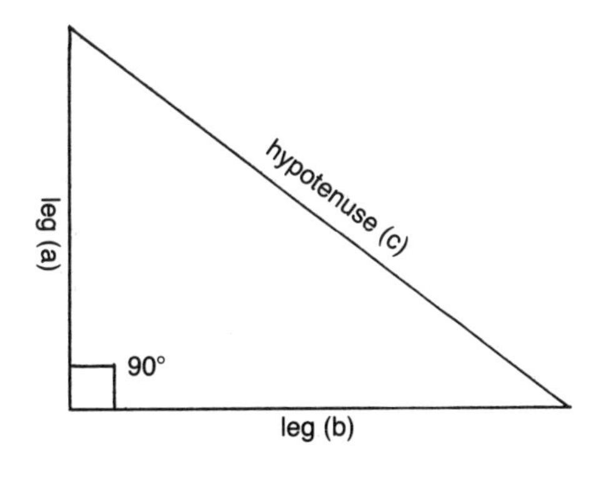

Figure 18. A right triangle: one of its three angles is 90°.

90°. The number of degrees in the other two angles of a right triangle always adds up to another 90°. The three angles of any triangle in Euclidean geometry always total 180°.

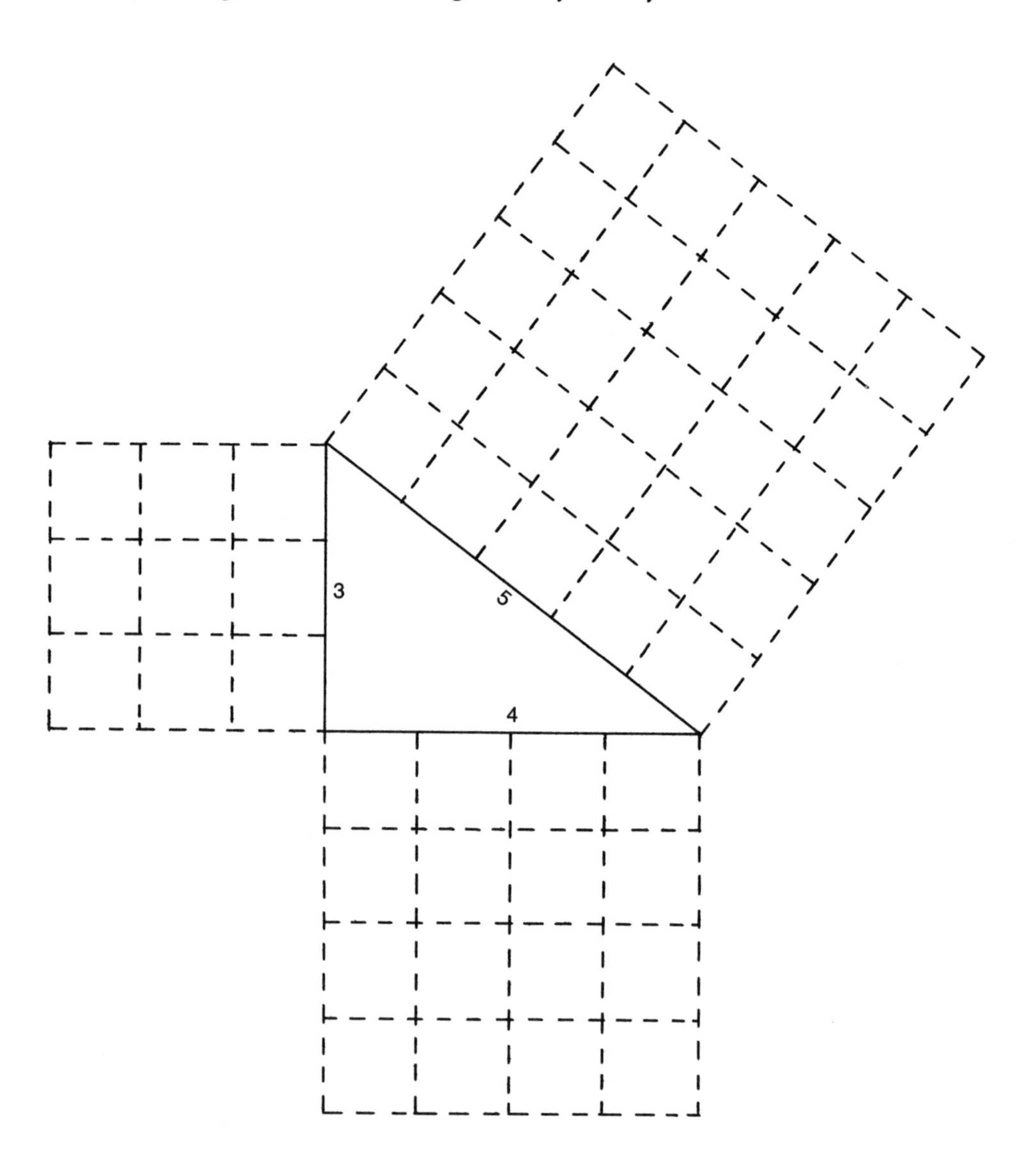

Figure 19. The sum of the squares of the two legs of a right triangle equals the square of the hypotenuse.

The side of a right triangle that is opposite the right angle is called the "hypotenuse." It is always the longest side in such a triangle. The other two sides are called the "legs" of the triangle.

Around 550 B.C., the Greek mathematician Pythagoras discovered that if the lengths of the legs of a right triangle are known, the length of the hypotenuse can be calculated. The "Pythagorean theorem" states that the sum of the squares of the two legs equals the square of the hypotenuse. This is usually written as an equation:

$$a^2 + b^2 = c^2$$

For example, if a right triangle has legs of 3 inches and 4 inches, then its hypotenuse will be 5 inches.

$$\begin{aligned} (3)^2 &= 9 \\ (4)^2 &= 16 \\ & \overline{25} = (5)^2 \end{aligned}$$

The same hypotenuse (5 inches long) can have legs of many different lengths as long as the sum of their squares adds up to 25. One leg may be very short, such as one inch long, and the other almost as long as the hypotenuse itself (it would be about 4.9 inches long).

$$\begin{aligned} (1)^2 &= 1 \\ (4.9)^2 &= 24 \\ & \overline{25} = (5)^2 \end{aligned}$$

As you can see in Figure 20, there are all sorts of possible combinations.

Although a right triangle is not an exact representation of the

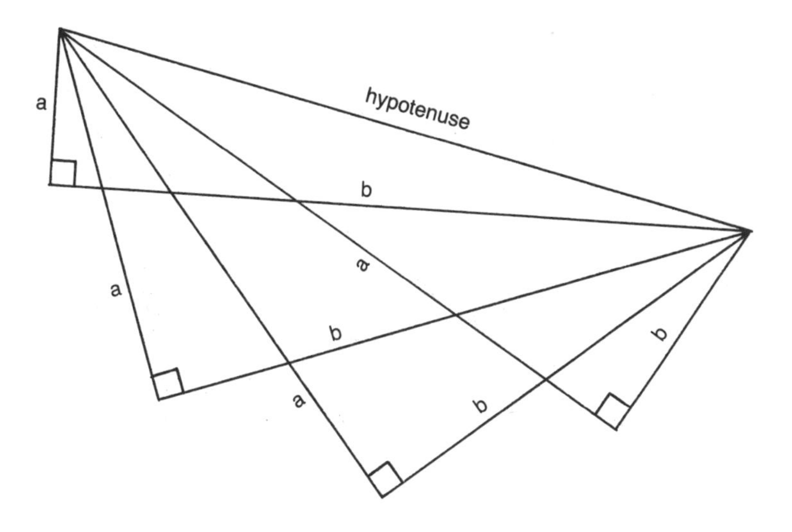

Figure 20. The same hypotenuse can have legs of many different lengths.

relationship between space-time intervals and space and time, we can use it as an illustration. Let us call one leg of a right triangle "time" and the other leg "space." That is, the time leg is the period of time between two observed events and the space leg is the distance between them. The hypotenuse is the interval between these two events in space-time.

Like the hypotenuse in our right triangle, no matter how the legs vary in length, the interval never changes. It is an absolute quantity. Each observer witnessing the two events will measure the time and distance between the two events in terms of his own frame of reference. These measurements will depend upon the observer's motion relative to the events, and therefore may vary from one observer to the other. But the space-time interval—the hypotenuse—between the two events will not vary.

Of course, not all hypotenuses of right triangles have the

same length. And not all intervals in space-time are the same. But for any given interval in space-time, there can be many different space and time measurements, just as there are many different combinations of leg lengths for any given hypotenuse. The interval itself does not change.

In the thought experiment about the lightning flashes, both you and the train passenger made measurements, each from your own frame of reference. These measurements differed. However, if either of you took these measurements and put them into equations given by the theory of relativity, you would both get the same space-time interval between the two events. This interval is an absolute quantity in space-time even though two observers may see it in different ways.

Einstein's theory and its application to the space-time continuum thus removed the influence of local frames of reference from the real picture of the universe. As we have seen, the theory was revolutionary in all its aspects. The big question,

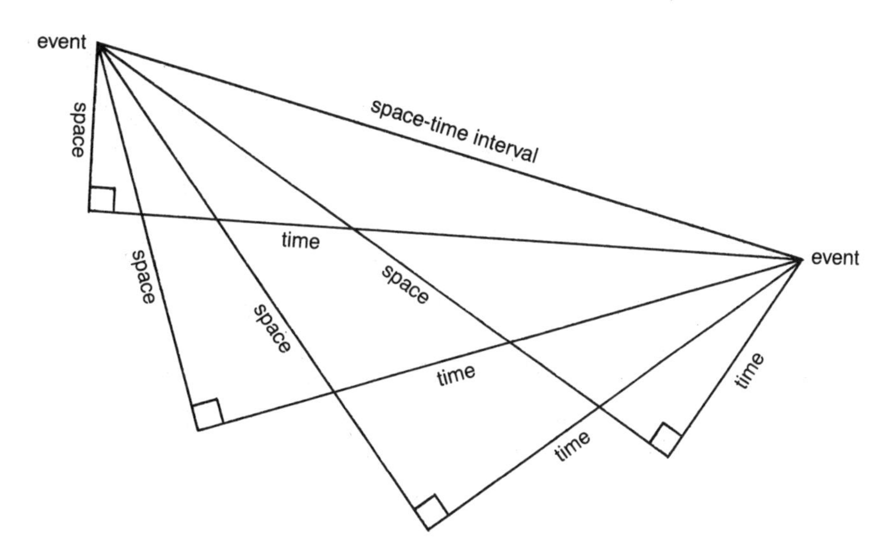

Figure 21. There can be many different space and time measurements for any given interval in space-time.

then, was: does it work? Einstein was so confident that it did work that he proposed three tests. These, he said, would prove that his theory was able to explain and predict phenomena which no other theory had been able to do before. Let us now look at these three tests of the theory of relativity.

7

The Extra Forty-three Seconds of Arc

IF A BAR MAGNET is placed under a sheet of plain white paper and iron filings are sprinkled on the paper, the filings will fall in a definite pattern. They will fall along the lines of the magnetic field created by the magnet, making the field visually detectable. This simple experiment is performed in most elementary physics classes to illustrate the concept of a magnetic field. Note that the magnet does not "attract" the filings *to* it but instead creates a magnetic field in the space *around* it. It is the magnetic field that acts upon the filings and makes them behave in a certain manner. The magnetic field is a physical reality and has a specific structure which can be seen on the white paper. The properties of the space around the magnet have been altered by the presence of the magnet itself. There are equations that describe these properties and how they affect objects such as the iron filings which have entered the field.

Only certain types of matter are magnetic, but all material objects have gravitational fields around them. We cannot see these gravitational fields, but we can detect them by their effect on objects moving through them just as we detected the structure of the magnetic field from the way filings lined up on the piece of paper. According to the theory of relativity, the gravitational field surrounding any object in the universe warps or curves the space-time around it. This curvature affects the path of any other object moving in the same region.

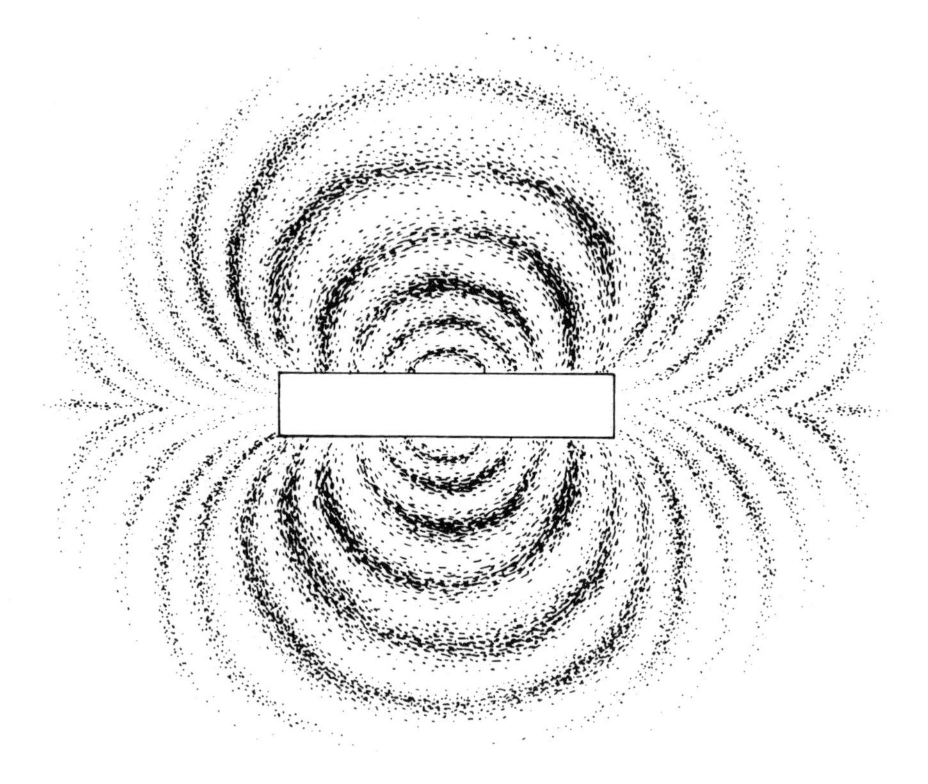

Figure 22. Iron filings outline the magnetic field of a bar magnet.

All objects moving in space follow what is called a "geodesic" path. A geodesic is defined as the shortest route possible between two points in a given region. On a flat surface such as this page, the shortest distance between two points is a straight line. You can place a wooden ruler on the line between points A and B in Figure 23 to prove that it is not curved in any way. The line is the geodesic between A and B—that is, it is the shortest path possible.

If an airplane were going to follow a geodesic path flying from Chicago, Illinois, to London, England, what route would

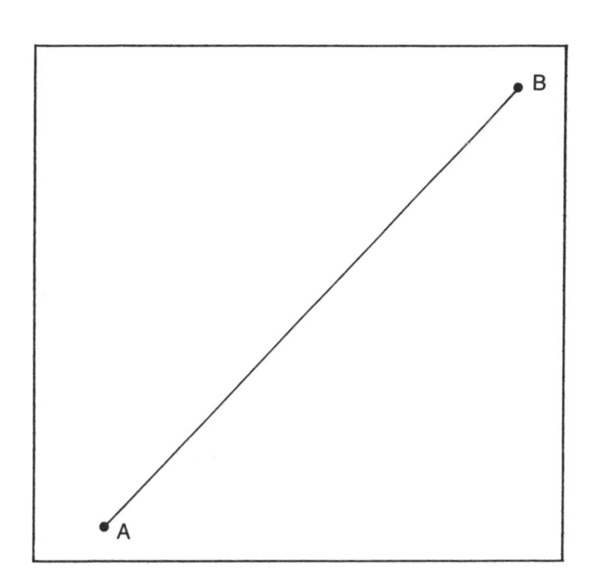

Figure 23. On a flat piece of paper, the shortest distance between points A and B is a straight line.

it take? Using a ruler, trace such a path on a map of the world. You will find that a straight line between Chicago and London goes through Detroit and Halifax, Nova Scotia. But the plane won't follow that path. It will fly a more northerly route, passing close to the tip of Greenland and crossing part of Ireland before landing in London. On the map this is a curved path and is certainly longer than the straight-line path that you laid out with your ruler.

Now look at a globe of the world. Measure the distance of both routes with a thin strip of paper or a piece of string held against the globe. You will see why this northern route is taken. On the globe it is much shorter than the one you traced first on the map. (See Figure 24.) The geometry or shape of the map is different from that of the globe. The map is flat, whereas the globe is spherical. The globe is, of course, much closer to the real shape of the earth. The path of the airplane follows this spherical shape. Within the frame of reference of this geometrical shape, the plane moves along a geodesic line, the shortest path possible between the two points, the two cities.

Looking at the globe, we can easily see why the airplane

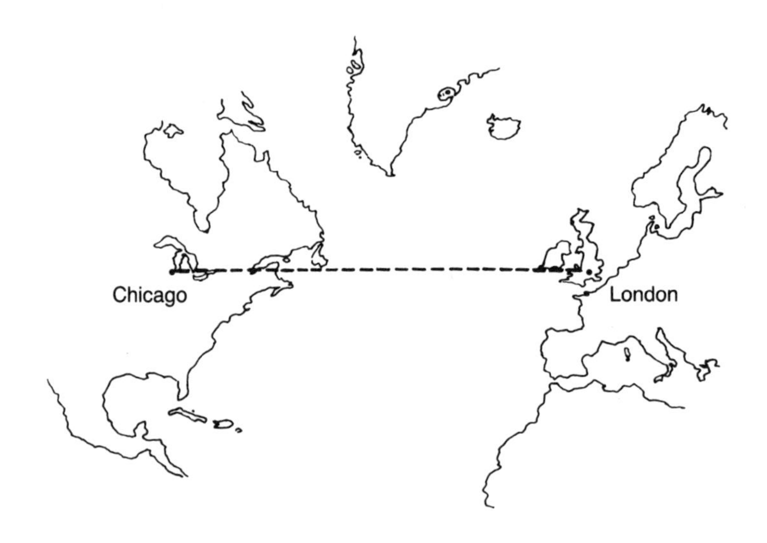

Figure 24. A straight line drawn on a map between Chicago and London does not cross the same areas as the geodesic route of an airplane. The airplane flies along a curved route from Chicago to London.

must follow a path dictated by the spherical shape of the earth. However, we cannot *see* the warped or curved space-time around an object such as the sun. Therefore, we cannot *visually* determine the shape of the space-time in that region.

There are complicated equations in Einstein's general theory of relativity which express the relationship between a massive object and its effect on the shape of the space-time around it. There are other equations which tell us how something will move in this curved space-time. This second group of equations describes the geodesic paths mathematically. Rather than use the equations that are so complex, let us use a comparison with something familiar to us in order to understand this concept.

Imagine a very large mattress made of soft foam rubber. If you place a small marble on it, the indentation will be very slight. But if you put a ten-pound ball on it, the ball will sink deeply into the mattress. The area around the ball will slope downward under the ball rather than staying level. If you roll the marble past the sunken ball, it will follow the new curvature of the mattress rather than the original flat plane.

If an ant were walking along the mattress, it, too, would follow the curvature made by the heavy ball. The ant might think that it was following a straight path, but it would be a lot easier going toward the ball (downhill) than climbing away from it. If the ant were intelligent enough, it might even think that some mysterious force was pulling it toward the ball and keeping it from moving away from the ball.

Like the mattress, the space-time continuum is warped or curved by the presence of massive objects. When something enters these warped regions, its path is affected by the curvature. The object may "feel" as though it is being dragged inward by the gravitational force of the massive body, but it is actually the curvature of the space-time continuum that dictates the object's motion. In other words the presence of matter in

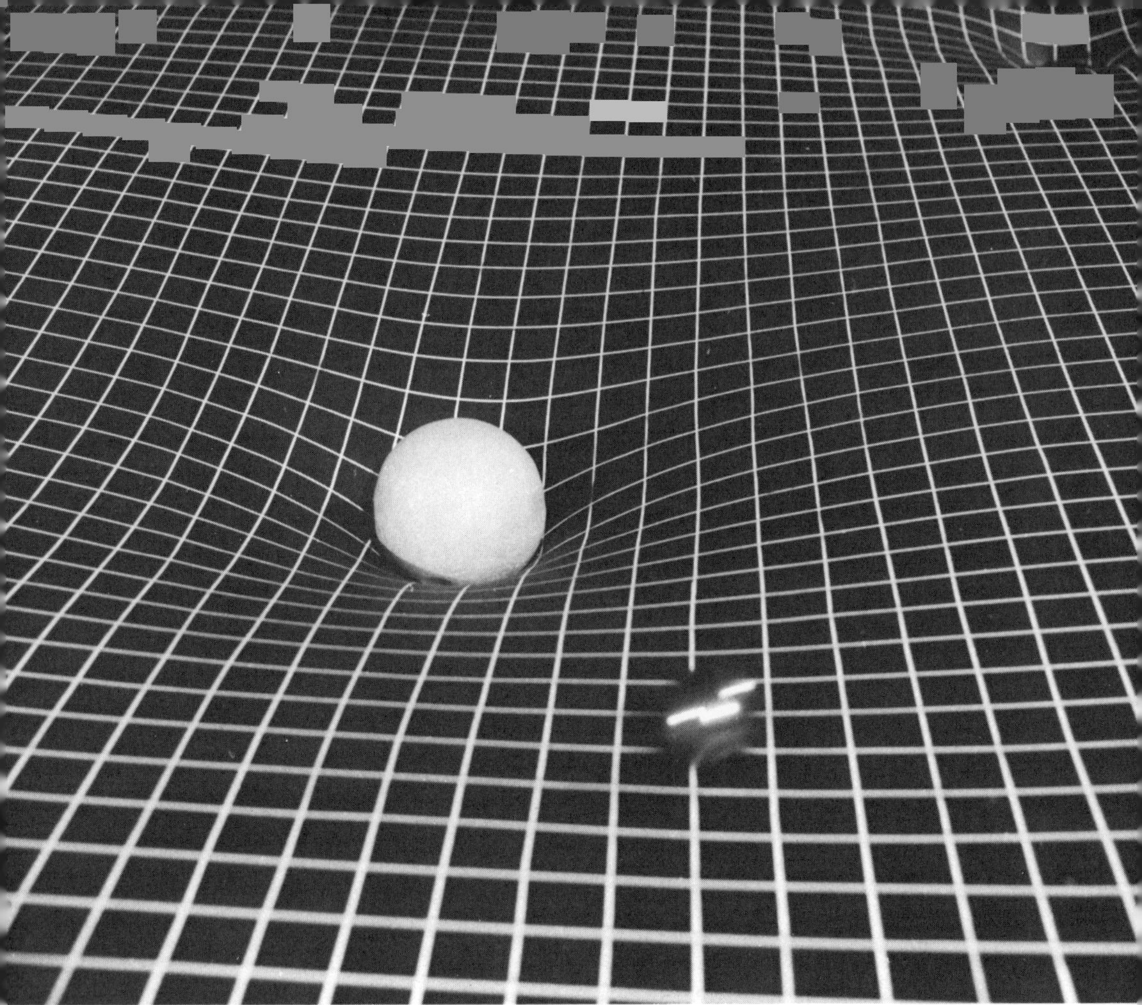

A representation of space-time: massive bodies warp or distort the space-time continuum. Less massive bodies moving near such distortions will follow the new curvature. It is the curvature of the space-time that determines their paths.

the space-time continuum dictates how that space-time will be curved, what geometry or shape it will have. The shape of the space-time in which matter finds itself affects the path that matter will follow.

According to the theory of relativity, every object in the universe has a gravitational field which warps or curves the space-time in its immediate vicinity and thereby influences the path that any other object will take in that region. The more massive the object is and the more its mass is concentrated or pushed together, the stronger its gravitational field will be.

The gravitational field of the sun, for example, is stronger than that of the earth because the sun is so much more massive. If the sun (or any other object) were reduced to one-half its size but kept the same mass, its gravitational field at its surface would be four times stronger. A reduction to one-third its original size (with the same mass) would result in a ninefold gravitational increase at the surface. On the earth, such an increase would mean that we and everything else would weigh proportionally more. A 100-pound object on the earth's surface would weigh 900 pounds on an earth reduced to one-third the earth's present size, assuming that the smaller earth had the same amount of matter (mass) in it.

The stronger the gravitational field around an object, the more the space-time will be curved. The space-time around the sun, for example, is much more curved than that around the earth. Because the sun's gravitational field extends throughout

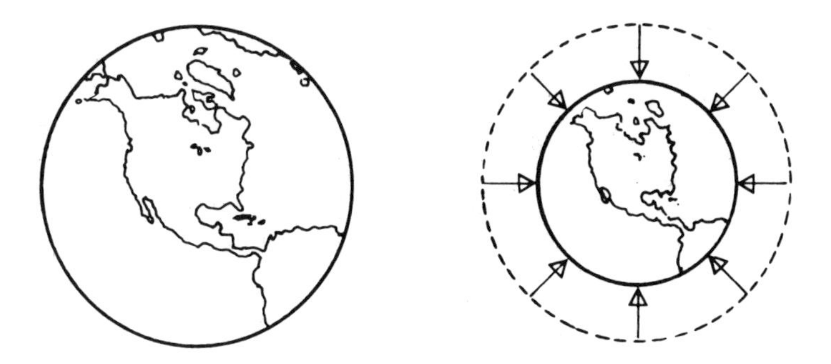

Figure 25. If the earth's mass were compacted to one-third its present volume, your weight would increase nine times.

Sir Isaac Newton (1642–1727).

Yerkes Observatory photo

the solar system, it curves the space-time far out beyond Pluto. The motions of all the planets are determined by the geometry or shape of the space-time in the solar system. Their geodesic paths are orbits around the sun. If the sun were suddenly removed, the space-time in the solar system would be much flatter. The planetary paths would no longer be as curved as they are now. The planets would instead travel in almost straight lines under the influence of the much flatter space-time. This is much like what would happen to the ant's path on the mattress if the heavy ball were removed.

The concept that warped space-time determines planetary orbits was a radical departure from previously held theories, especially those about gravitation. Nearly three centuries ago the famous English scientist Isaac Newton described gravity as an attractive force between any two objects in the universe. This "force-at-a-distance," he said, pulled the objects toward each other with a strength that depended upon the combined (multiplied) mass of the objects and their distance from each other. The greater the mass and the smaller the distance, the stronger the force of gravitation. This was Newton's Universal Law of Gravitation.

Newton derived his law of gravitation and its mathematical formulas from observations of the world around him. He did not try to explain why such a force existed or what it was. The

The Apollo 15 Command and Service Modules in orbit around the moon. Photograph was taken from the Lunar Module just before it reunited with the Command Module.

NASA photo

law was believed to be correct because it described and predicted observable events. It was used successfully to calculate the orbits of comets and asteroids. New planets were discovered with the use of Newton's equations.

The trajectories of the Apollo spacecraft, which went to the moon in the 1960's and 1970's, were calculated from Newton's laws and formulas. For such purposes, Newtonian theory is adequate because the gravitational fields in which these objects move are relatively weak. The space-time in the solar system is not warped or curved very much. It is almost flat and therefore the geodesic of the objects moving in it is very close to a straight line. The classical "flat" (or "plane") geometry of the Greek mathematician Euclid can be used. Newton's theory was based upon Euclidean geometry.

With the use of Newton's formulas, the orbits of the planets could be successfuly predicted. This had been a goal of astronomers from ancient times. Other systems of calculating planetary

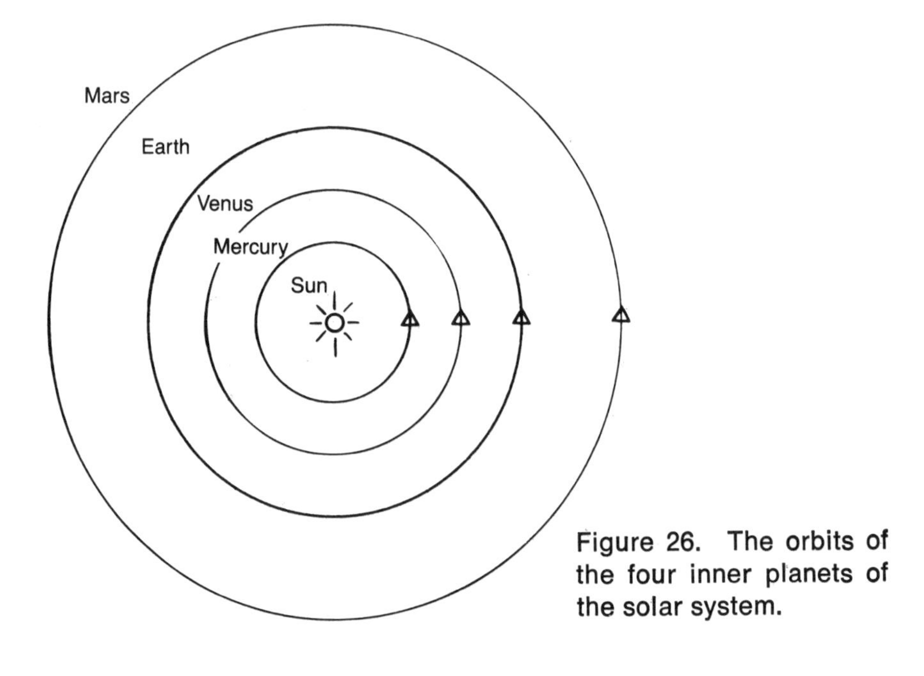

Figure 26. The orbits of the four inner planets of the solar system.

NASA photo

Halley's comet: Edmund Halley, using Newton's law of gravitation, successfully predicted the date when this comet would appear again in its orbit around the sun.

orbits had been devised before the seventeenth century, but they had been hampered by the belief that the planets moved in circular orbits. (Of course, the ancient theories had these orbits going around the earth, not the sun.) In ancient times a circle was believed to be a perfect shape and therefore was considered the only one good enough for the heavenly bodies to follow. But the observed locations of the planets did not fit the predicted ones when such predictions were based upon circular orbits. Efforts to correct these discrepancies while still preserving the perfect circular orbits led to more and more complicated systems. It was not until the seventeenth century that such systems were finally abandoned. The weight of evidence was clearly against them. All observations and mathematical calculations showed that the planets move in elliptical orbits.

An ellipse is an oval shape, somewhat like an egg. Unlike a circle, it is longer in one dimension than in the one perpendicular to it. The longer dimension is called the "major axis" and the smaller one is called the "minor axis." The difference in length between the major and minor axes can differ from one ellipse to another. The greater the difference, the more elongated the ellipse becomes. A circle can be thought of as an ellipse in which the two axes are equal.

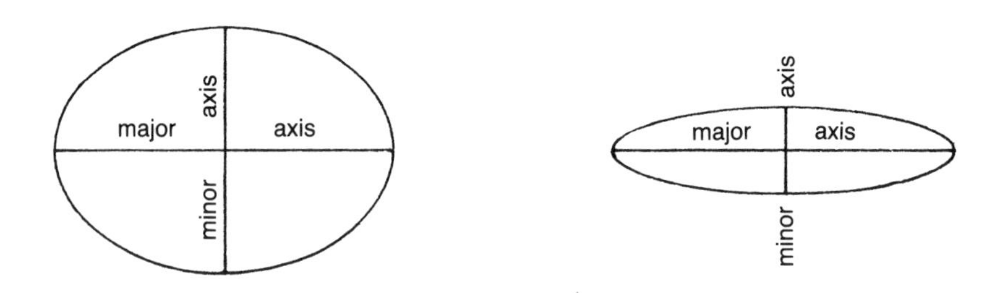

Figure 27. Two ellipses: Although the major axis of both is the same length, the difference in the length of the minor axes makes their shapes different.

The orbits of the planets are ellipses, but the differences between their major and minor axes are very small. It takes very careful measurements of the planets' positions to establish the elliptical shape of their orbits. Because the orbits are so close in shape to a circle, they are usually drawn that way in textbooks. Most of these illustrations also put the sun in the center of the orbits, although this is not an accurate representation either.

The sun is not at the center of any of the planetary orbits. It is located on the major axis slightly off to one side of the center. Therefore, as each planet revolves around the sun its distance from the sun varies. For example, the earth is closest to the sun on January 2 every year. At that time it is approximately 91.4 million miles away. On that date the earth is at the "perihelion" point in its orbit. Six months later, around July 2, the earth is at its farthest point from the sun, or 94.5 million miles away. It is then at "aphelion." We usually say that the sun is about 93 million miles away, but that is just an average figure for the whole year. (It is about that far away on April 3 and October 1.)

When Isaac Newton was developing his theory in the seventeenth century, he knew that the gravitational attraction of the planets on each other would disturb their orbital paths around

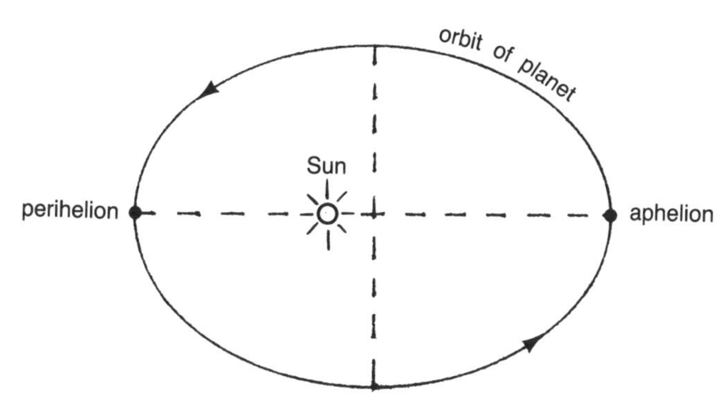

Figure 28. The sun is not at the center of any of the planetary orbits.

the sun. His equations predicted such disturbances, or "perturbations." It was not until the early nineteenth century that the French mathematician Pierre Simon de Laplace was able to compute just how much each planet's orbit was disturbed by the gravitational disturbances from the other planets. He used Newton's equations to do this. Although it was a very minute amount, Laplace knew that one of the major effects of these gravitational disturbances was the very slight but constant rotation of each planet's orbit.

For each planet, the perihelion and aphelion points are slowly revolving around the sun, taking many thousands of years to make one complete revolution. The farther away the planet is from the sun, the slower this revolution is. However, even with Mercury, the amount is so very small that it is only a tiny fraction of a degree (of a circle) per *century*. This is true for all the planetary orbits.

Mathematicians divide a circle into 360 degrees. An angle of one degree is 1/360 of a circle. For more accurate measurements, each of these degrees is divided into 60 "minutes of arc" and each of the minutes of arc is divided into 60 "seconds of arc." Every degree of a circle can therefore be divided into 3600 seconds of arc (60 x 60). There are 1,296,000 seconds of arc in a full circle. (Do not confuse minutes and seconds of arc with time periods. It is unfortunate that the same words and units of division are used.)

Laplace's computations showed that the amount of rotation of any of the planets' orbits was measured in seconds of arc per century. He was able to compute these tiny changes, but it was not until the middle of the nineteenth century that observational techniques were refined enough to enable astronomers to detect them. The perihelion and aphelion points of the inner planets (Mercury, Venus, and Mars) were found to be very slowly moving around the sun just as Laplace had predicted.

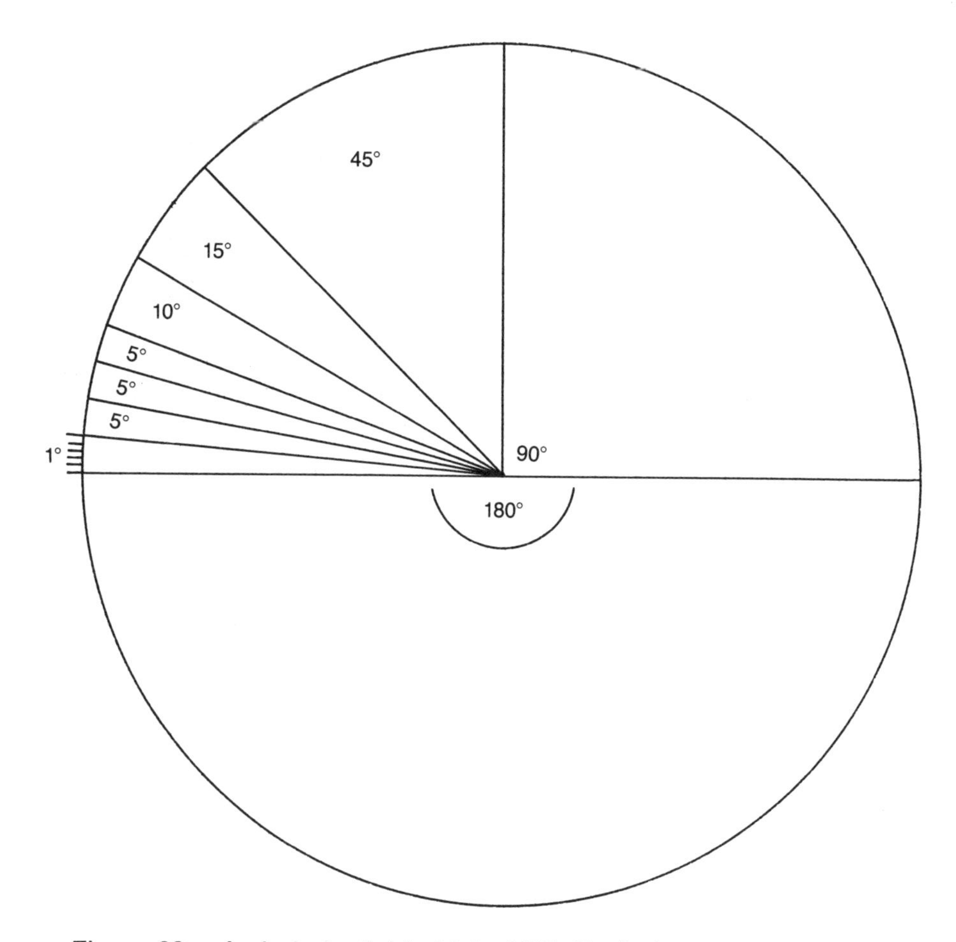

Figure 29. A circle is divided into 360°. Each degree is divided into 60 minutes of arc. Each minute of arc is divided into 60 seconds of arc. (Minutes and seconds are too small to be shown.)

For Venus and Mars, the amount observed and the amount predicted were in close enough agreement to assume that the differences were due to observational error.

But this was not true for Mercury. It was found that Mercury's orbit was rotating 43 seconds of arc per century faster than Laplace had predicted. This was too great a discrepancy

JPL-NASA photo

The planet Mercury photographed by cameras aboard the Mariner 10 spacecraft from a distance of 124,000 miles (200,000 kms). The largest of the craters are about 124 miles (200 kms) across.

to attribute to observational error. Some scientists even thought that there was an unknown planet between Mercury and the sun that was responsible, but despite a long and intense search for such a body, none was ever found.

When Einstein was developing his general theory of relativity in the early twentieth century, this extra 43 seconds of arc was still unexplained. Einstein felt that this might be an excellent area in which to test his theory and therefore he applied his equations to the problem.

Mercury is the closest planet to the sun and travels at the greatest speed around it. In Newtonian theory, these factors are not considered important; Mercury's motion should be basically the same as any other planet's. But according to the theory of relativity, an object's path through space-time is determined by the curvature of that space-time. The sun's gravitational field is strongest nearest the sun and therefore Mercury moves in a much more curved space-time than any of the other planets.

Newton's formulas are not sufficient to explain the entire amount of rotation of Mercury's orbit. They do not take into consideration the effect of the much stronger gravitational field

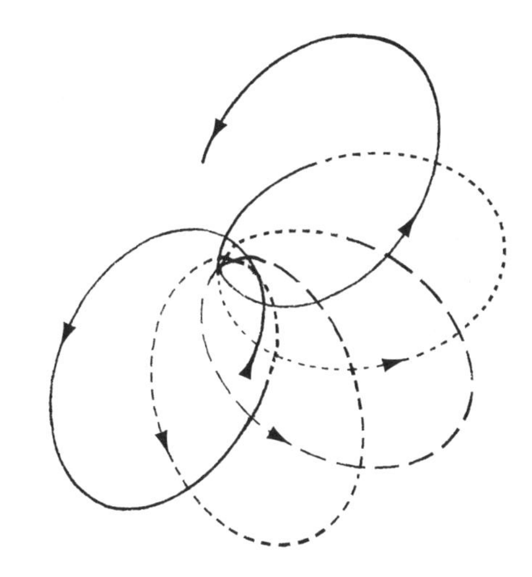

Figure 30. Mercury's orbit describes a rosette pattern rather than a stationary ellipse. (Diagram is greatly exaggerated.)

JPL-NASA phc

The planet Venus, photographed by cameras aboard the Mariner 10 spacecraft from a distance of 450,000 miles (720,000 km). Light and dark areas both are thick clouds covering the planet.

and the resulting curvature of the space-time continuum. Einstein's equations as presented in his theory of relativity are necessary here in order to obtain a true picture. When these equations are used, the extra 43 seconds of arc are fully accounted for.

This was a major triumph for the theory of relativity. Its reputation was further enhanced in 1960 when it was discovered that the extra eight seconds of arc per century observed in Venus's orbit were not due to observational error as had been originally believed, but were almost completely accounted for by Einstein's equations.

Solving the mystery of the 43 seconds of arc was the first of three tests that Einstein believed would prove the validity of his theory. In this test he took a problem that had been worked on by scientists before him. In the other two he predicted results in new areas of research which had yet to be investigated. It was these tests which showed the world what a genius he was.

The Bending of Light

EINSTEIN'S THEORY OF RELATIVITY had successfully explained the extra 43 seconds of arc in Mercury's orbital rotation. His equations had solved that mystery. This, however, was not enough to establish the theory as completely different from those which had come before it. If the theory could predict some new phenomena which had not been thought of before, then it would be hailed as a truly revolutionary change in scientific thought.

With this in mind, Einstein searched for other tests which would prove the accuracy of his new theory. He knew that because the gravitational field within the solar system is relatively weak, the space-time continuum there is practically flat. Any measurement to detect the warping of space-time in this region would be extremely small and would require very sensitive instruments. Until the twentieth century, such methods of detection were not available. Our technology was not advanced enough to measure successfully even the deviations caused by the gravitational field of the sun. They were too small. If a genius like Newton had thought of such a concept as warped space-time, he would never have been able to prove it, and verified predictions are the true tests of any theory. Because the space-time in the solar system is almost flat, his equations are still usable today when determining most of the motions of objects within the solar system.

However, Newton limited his theory of gravity to material objects. According to his Universal Law of Gravitation, only material objects were affected by the gravitational attraction of a massive body. Light rays were not believed to be affected by gravity. They were thought to travel through space in straight lines. From all scientific observations of the world and especially of the sky, this certainly appeared to be the way light behaved. No one imagined that it could behave any differently.

The theory of relativity, however, says that anything moving through the space-time continuum will naturally follow the shortest path allowable, a geodesic. This path is dictated by the shape or geometry of the space-time in which the motion is taking place. In a region where the space-time is curved or warped, this path will be warped or curved. And the more the space-time is curved, the more the path will deviate from a straight line. This applies to everything moving in this space-time continuum, including light rays. We would therefore see the path of a light ray as following a geodesic, according to the theory of relativity.

If this is true, then a light ray when passing a massive object should appear to deviate from its straight-line path through space just as a material object would have its path bent or curved in such a region. The more massive the object, the more the path of the light ray would appear to be bent.

This was a radical departure from the classical Newtonian theory of gravitation. It was a new concept which had never been considered before. If such a deviation in the path of a light ray could be detected, it would be an important proof of Einstein's theory. It would show the superiority of the theory of relativity over Newton's Universal Law of Gravitation. Newton's law could never explain such a phenomenon.

Einstein knew that he needed a much more massive body

than the earth to be able to prove his theory. Even the most sensitive instruments available would not be able to detect any deviation that a light ray might take from a straight line here on earth. He therefore looked to the sun. The sun contains 99 percent of all the mass in the solar system and is therefore a much more massive body than any of the planets. It is 332,000 times more massive than the earth. The gravitational field of the sun is therefore much stronger than that of the earth or any of the other planets. And it is strongest in the region nearest the sun.

The space-time continuum is therefore much more curved very close to the sun than it is anywhere else in the solar sys-

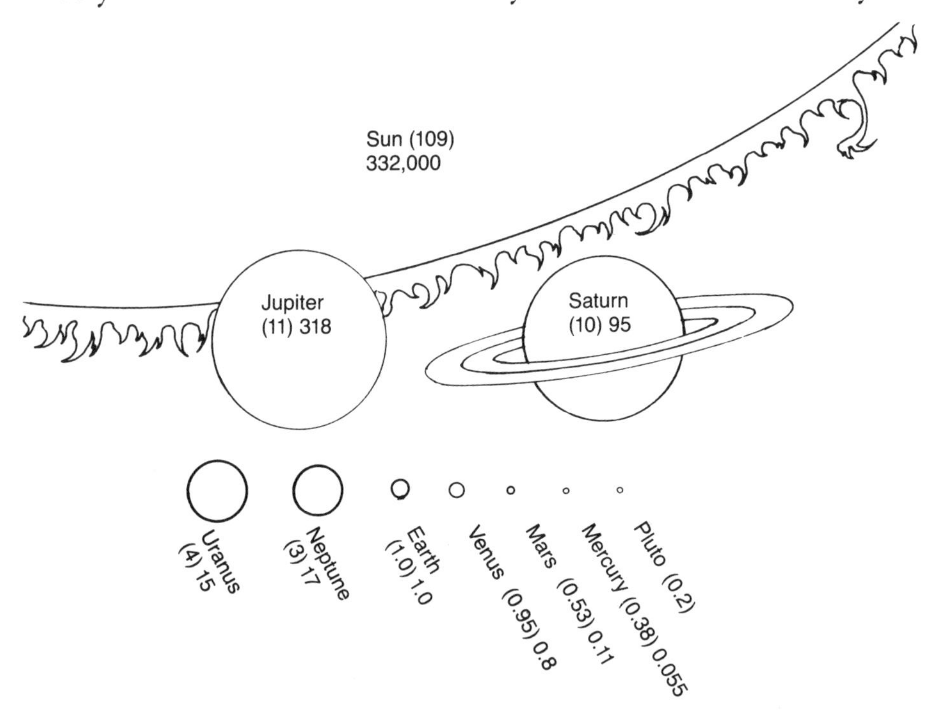

Figure 31. The relative sizes of the sun and planets. Number in parentheses compares the diameter of each object with that of earth. The second number compares the mass of each object with that of earth.

tem. That is why Mercury's orbit is affected more than the orbits of the other planets.

With the use of his equations, Einstein was able to determine just how much the space-time continuum is curved close to the sun. He then predicted that a ray of light passing through this warped space-time would have its path curved or bent by a detectable amount. This amount, Einstein said, was 1.75 seconds of arc.

As we saw in Chapter Six and as shown in Figure 32, this is an extremely small angle. Very precise measurements would be necessary to detect such a minute deviation. Let us remember that if Newton had suspected that such a phenomenon was possible, he would never have been able to measure it with the instruments available to him in the seventeenth century.

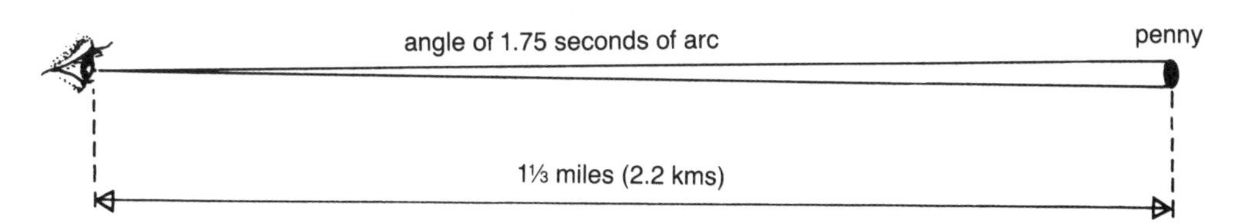

Figure 32. If we make a triangle with a base the width of a penny and legs 1⅓ miles (2.2 kms) long, the tiny angle opposite the penny will be about 1.75 seconds of arc.

The ray of light to be measured would have to come from a distant star beyond the sun. However, we cannot normally see the stars during the daytime because of the intense glare of the sun blocking out all other light. How could the path of any starlight ever be measured as it passed closed to the sun?

Einstein suggested taking the measurements during a total solar eclipse. At that time the moon passes directly between the earth and the sun and casts its shadow upon a small area of the earth. The brilliant rays from the sun which are traveling toward that region on the earth are blocked off for a few minutes and all that can be seen is the magnificent solar corona.

During the period of totality when only the corona is visible, the sky becomes so dark that stars are visible. Photographs of these stars can be taken at that time so that their exact positions in the sky can be measured. If the light from a star has deviated from a straight line, the star will not appear in the usual position in the sky relative to the other stars around it. It will be 1.75 seconds of arc "out of place."

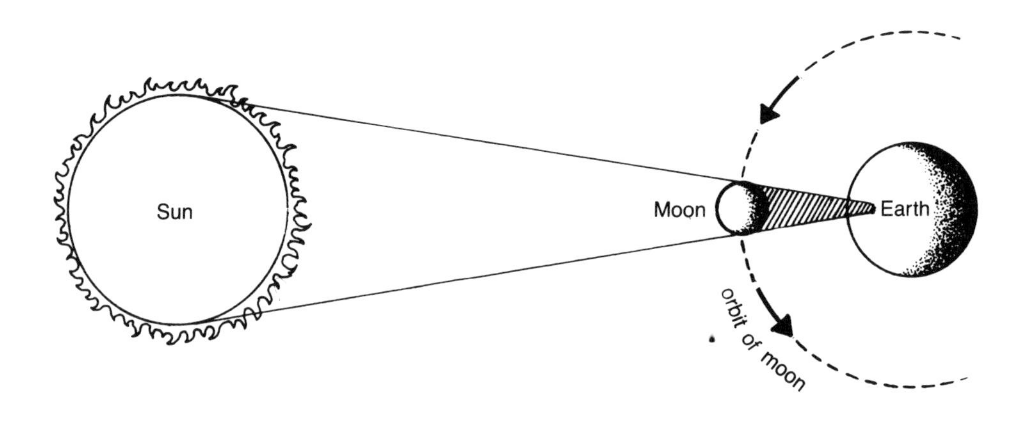

Figure 33. When the moon passes directly between the sun and the earth, the moon's shadow falls upon a small area of the earth. For a very few minutes that area experiences darkness.

However, the stars that are seen during a total solar eclipse are not the same stars that are seen the following night. At night we see the stars that are on the same side of the sun as we are. During the eclipse, we see the stars on the other side of the sun. That is why we normally cannot see them. In order to see these stars again, we must wait until the earth has moved

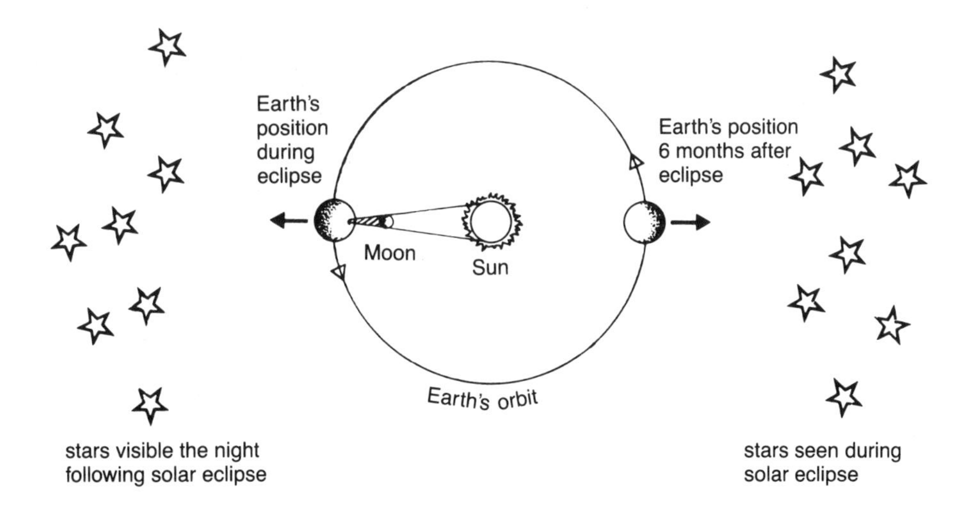

Figure 34. The stars seen during a total solar eclipse are not the same stars that are seen the following night. The stars seen during the eclipse will be in the night sky six months later when the earth moves to the other side of its orbit.

around the sun to the other side of its orbit. The stars that we saw during the eclipse will then be visible in our night sky.

Today solar eclipses do not happen very frequently and when they do they are often visible only in the most inconvenient locations on earth. Einstein presented his theory in 1916, but he had to wait until 1919 for the next suitable solar eclipse. In May of that year, a group of British astronomers journeyed to a small island off the west coast of Africa to witness and photograph a total solar eclipse. The major purpose of this expedition was to photograph stars near the edge of the eclipsed sun so that their positions could be compared with their positions on photographs taken several months earlier.

When the measurements had been completed and compared with the earlier photographs, the light from these stars was found to have been deflected or bent by almost the exact amount predicted by Einstein's equations. When this news be-

Dearborn Observatory photo

Total solar eclipse: only the sun's corona is visible as the moon completely covers the solar disk.

came public, Einstein's theory was verified and it became internationally known. Later, improved methods of testing this same displacement of light reconfirmed the accuracy of his prediction.

We must be careful of how we interpret the observed deflection of light rays passing through gravitational fields. We

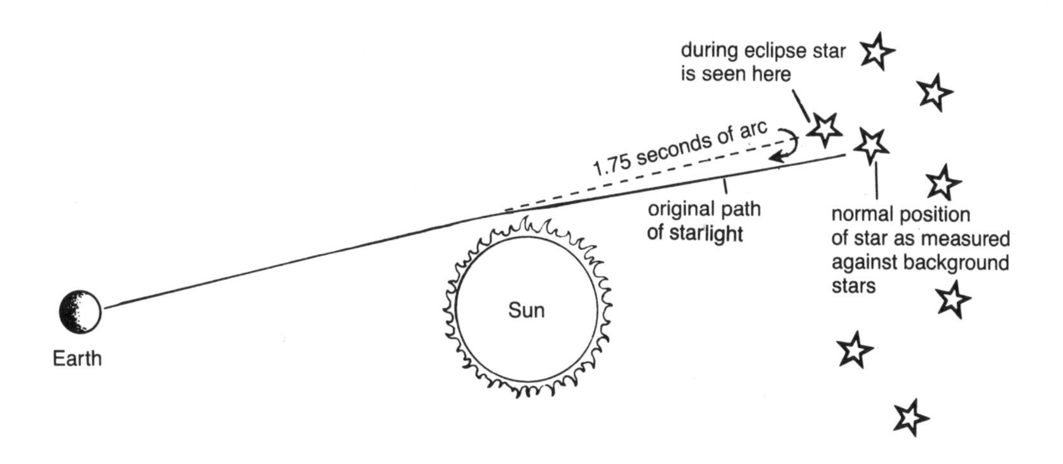

Figure 35. As observed from earth, the light from a distant star passing close to the sun will be 1.75 seconds of arc "out of place."

describe the light's path as we see it from the earth. By our measurements it is not following our definition of a straight line. We say it is not following the shortest path through space. Our frame of reference for a straight line comes from the curvature of the space-time continuum around the earth.

The sun is a very massive body by terrestrial standards, but there are other stars that have much more mass and, therefore, much more powerful gravitational fields. The space-time around them is warped to a much greater degree than the space-time around the sun. An object or a light ray in such a region would follow a geodesic that was much more curved than anything near the sun. A light ray as seen from the earth would be deflected by a greater angle than a light ray passing the sun.

Using Einstein's theory and equations, physicists in 1939 suggested the possibility of a star so massive and with so strong a gravitational field that it would actually bend or deflect a ray of light 180°. That is, light passing by such a star would be bent back upon itself and would never be able to leave the vicinity of the star again. This would also be true of any material object that came within the powerful gravitational field of this star. Because no light or other radiation could ever escape from such a star, it could not be seen. For this reason it was called a "black hole."

Although such stars were considered theoretically possible in 1939, it was not until the 1970's that astronomers started looking seriously for likely candidates far out in space. They have now located several stars which are believed to be accompanied by "black holes." Some astronomers also think that the centers of some galaxies, including our own, may possibly be gigantic black holes. Research in this area is very active today. It is a field that would have been completely unexplored without the theory of relativity as its foundation.

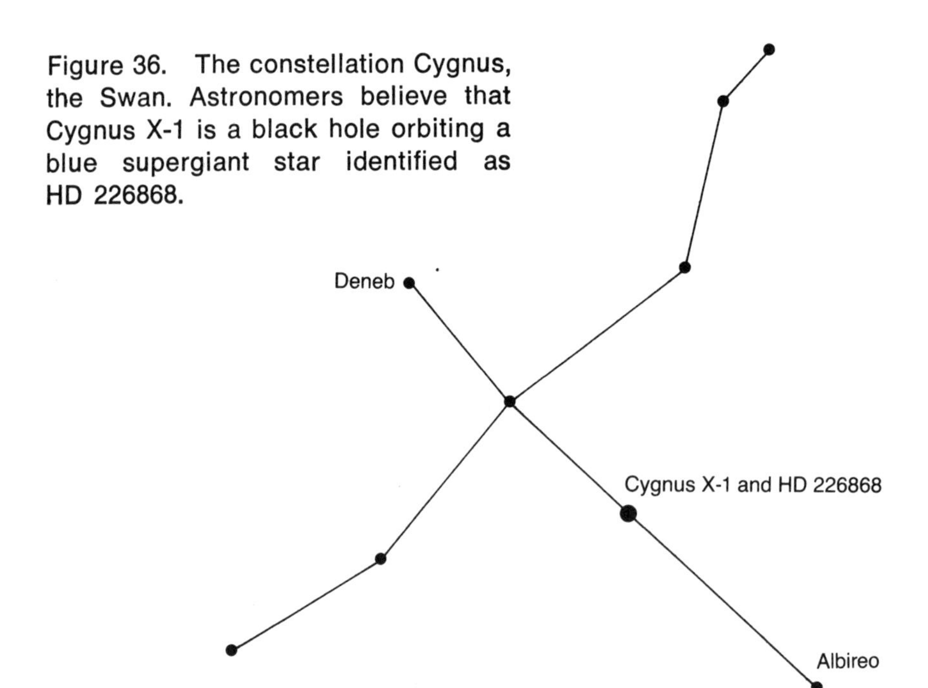

Figure 36. The constellation Cygnus, the Swan. Astronomers believe that Cygnus X-1 is a black hole orbiting a blue supergiant star identified as HD 226868.

The Measure of Time

A GRAVITATIONAL FIELD changes the shape of the space-time continuum. That is its effect on the spatial dimensions. But how does it affect the time dimension? That, too, should be altered and, according to the theory of relativity, it is. A gravitational field causes time to slow down. The stronger the field, the slower time will pass. Your watch runs slower when you are on the street than it does when you are up in a tall building because you are closer to the earth when you are on the street, and, therefore, are within a stronger gravitational field. Of course, with the tools of measurement available to you, you could never detect any difference in the passage of time at the two locations. Even if you were out in space, far away from any gravitational field, your watch would tick off only about one billionth of a second more per month than it does here on earth.

Einstein could not physically measure this slowing down of time, but he was confident that it was a true phenomenon. In fact, it was the third prediction that he made to prove the accuracy of his equations and of his theory of relativity. However, at the time that he presented his theory, scientists did not have clocks accurate enough to measure the extremely small change involved. It was not until after Einstein's death in 1955 that a method of measuring such small units of time as billionths of a second was found. Let us see how this is done.

Light is a form of energy. It can be thought of as a series of waves, like the waves on the surface of the ocean. Some of the ocean waves are very small and come one after another in rapid succession. Others are very large and come much less frequently. Light waves behave the same way. The more frequent the light wave, the smaller it will be. Longer light waves come less frequently. When the light energy hits our eyes, our brains interpret the wavelength and frequency of the light in terms of color. We see the color red when longer light waves enter our eyes, and blue-violet when shorter ones are present. In between the red and blue-violet extremes, all the colors of the rainbow are represented. One color fades into the next as the wavelength changes.

If we increase the wavelength of the radiation energy beyond the longest red wavelength, it is no longer perceived as light. Our eyes cannot detect wavelengths longer than those

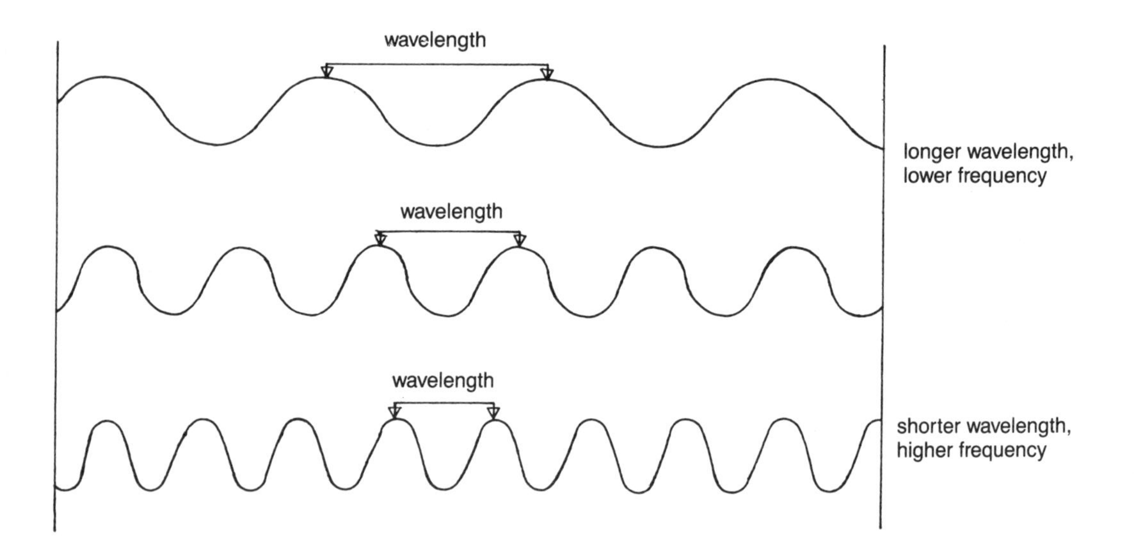

Figure 37. Wavelength is measured from crest to crest. Frequency is the number of waves passing a given point per second.

which produce the color red. But we have other senses that can. Wavelengths longer than light produce infrared energy radiation which we feel as heat. Microwave energy radiation (which we use in our microwave ovens) is manifested by still longer wavelengths.

Beyond the infrared and microwave wavelengths, we find radiation in the form of radio waves. The shorter radio waves are appropriately called "shortwave radio." As you can see in Figure 38, radio energy radiation gives us our familiar AM, FM, and TV broadcasts. We cannot sense this radio radiation as we can sense light or heat, but we have many instruments that can receive it for us and convert it into sound and light for our enjoyment.

Radiation with wavelengths shorter than that of blue light also is invisible. Just beyond the blue light limit, energy is in the form of ultraviolet radiation. Although we cannot feel or see this kind of radiation, we feel the effects of it if we stay out in the sun too long.

Shorter wavelengths than ultraviolet radiation are in the form of x-rays and gamma rays. You no doubt have been exposed to x-ray radiation for a very brief period of time when your dentist took x-rays of your teeth in order to detect cavities.

The entire range of wavelengths from the longest radio waves to the shortest gamma ray waves is called the "electromagnetic spectrum." All of these forms of energy travel at the speed of light and follow the same laws of nature that light does. A radio broadcast from the moon, for example, would reach the earth in the same time as a light beam would. And just like the light beam, the radio beam would be bent or deflected if it entered a strong gravitational field.

The sun and all the stars emit electromagnetic radiation at all of these wavelengths. X-rays and gamma rays on the one end of the spectrum and radio waves on the other end have

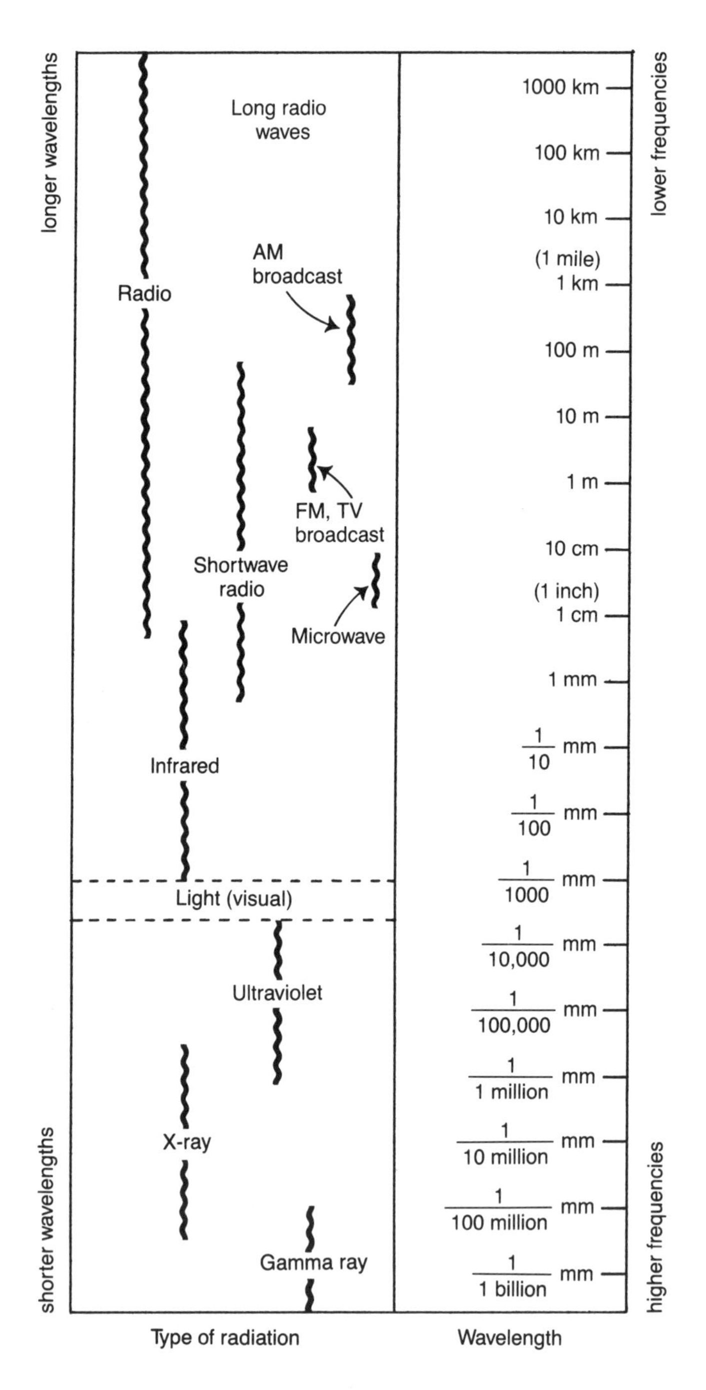

Figure 38. The electromagnetic spectrum.

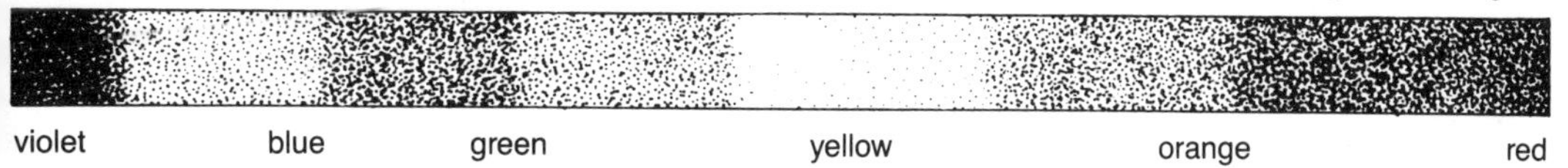

Figure 39. The spectrum of colors.

all been detected in outer space. Luckily, our atmosphere blocks most of this radiation from reaching us. Only light and radio waves plus a very small amount of the other kinds can penetrate this protective barrier. Most of them in any great quantity would be deadly to all life here on earth.

As you can see from the diagram, light is a very small portion of this spectrum. We usually use it in our examples about electromagnetic radiation because it is the kind of radiation with which we are most familiar. In fact, if the wavelength of any form of electromagnetic radiation is lengthened, we say that it is "red-shifted"—that is, it has moved toward the red end of the spectrum. We use this term even when speaking of radio waves or gamma waves, which are both far from the visual part of the spectrum. If the wavelength is shortened, it is said to have been "blue-shifted."

The wavelengths and frequencies of all of these forms of electromagnetic radiation have been measured with special instruments in laboratories. Frequency is usually given as the number of waves passing a particular point each second. Since the waves are very regular, their passing is like the ticking of a clock. Thus, electromagnetic radiation has been found to be an extremely accurate timekeeper. Our atomic clocks are based upon the frequency of the waves of a particular form of radiation. Frequency is a measure of time; it is a clock.

If Einstein's theory is correct, the frequency of the waves

of electromagnetic radiation coming from a source in a strong gravitational field should be slower than those from the same source in a weaker field. Here on earth, any changes in the strength of a gravitational field would be extremely tiny. Therefore, the red shift of any electromagnetic radiation within such a gravitational field would also be very small, as would any change in its frequency. It was found that the frequency of light waves is not fast enough to detect the very small difference there would be from such a change in the strength of a gravitational field. The light waves' frequency cannot divide a given period into small enough units to measure the minute changes. It would be like trying to measure your growth from babyhood to adulthood if the mile were the smallest unit of measurement available.

What was needed was a form of energy that had a much higher frequency, so that more precise units of time could be measured. Gamma rays, as we have seen, have much shorter wavelengths than light and therefore have higher frequencies. There are radioactive substances such as cobalt that give off gamma rays. Very accurate measurements of their wavelengths and frequencies have been made.

In 1959, two physicists at Harvard University measured the wavelength and frequency of gamma rays being emitted from a piece of radioactive cobalt on the ground floor and on the top floor of a 74-foot building. When the cobalt was on the ground floor, it was closer to the earth and therefore was in a stronger gravitational field. According to Einstein's theory, it should therefore radiate gamma-ray waves at a lower frequency. Its "clock" or rate of measuring time would be slowed down by the stronger gravitational field. When measurements were taken, it was found that the frequency was indeed slower on the ground floor by exactly the amount predicted by Einstein's equations. This experiment was repeated several years later and produced the same results.

If the frequency of the electromagnetic radiation slows down in a more powerful gravitational field, so do all other time processes. As we saw in Chapter Three, energy is another form of matter and, therefore, what affects energy will affect matter as well. Our biological clocks slow down in a stronger gravitational field. We do not age as quickly. Flowers grow more slowly. Iron rusts away more slowly.

Regardless of what timekeeping device we use to measure the passage of time, if its beat slows down, the passage of time for us also slows down. Today, atomic clocks are our most accurate means of measuring time. As accurate as they are, they would not give us the same time if they were on the sun (assuming that we could find some way to keep them from melting).

Because it was known that the gravitational field around the sun is much stronger than the one around the earth, astronomers tried to detect a difference in the frequency of the light coming from the sun as compared with light here on earth. However, they found that the difference was so small that it was overshadowed by other effects which caused similar variations in the sunlight.

Instead, they turned to stars with much stronger gravitational fields. The effect on the light coming from such stars would be stronger and more easily observed and measured. One type of such stars is called a "white dwarf." These are stars that are at the very end of their lives. They have used up all their fuel and are no longer able to produce nuclear reactions, which is the normal way stars create the energy that makes them shine. White dwarf stars shine only because they still have some energy left from their earlier days, but they are in the process of cooling off and will eventually become dark, cold objects in space.

When a star reaches the white dwarf stage, it collapses into a very small, dense object. It becomes a tiny star, not much bigger than the earth. Some white dwarf stars are even smaller than the earth. But because they still have the mass of an average star like the sun, the density of their material is enormous. A ball the size of a marble made of such compressed material would weigh about 30 tons or more here on earth.

As we saw in Chapter Seven, if an object retains its mass but is pushed into a smaller size, the strength of the gravitational field on its surface increases tremendously. In the example in Chapter Seven, the earth was compressed to only one-third its present size and yet a 100-pound person would weigh 900 pounds on such a small earth. In the case of the white dwarf, it has collapsed to a size many thousands of times smaller than its former volume. The strength of the gravitational field on its

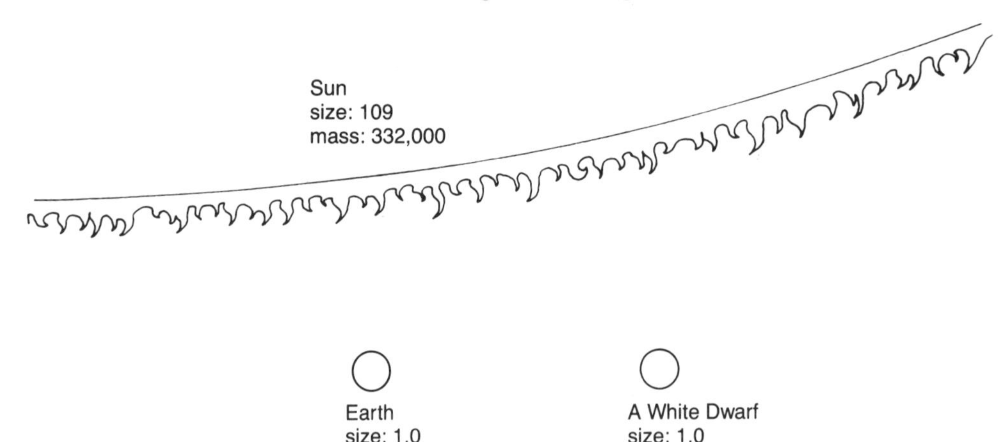

Figure 40. A comparison of the size and mass of the sun, the earth, and a white dwarf.

surface is therefore thousands of times stronger than before.

According to the theory of relativity, in the presence of such a powerful gravitational field the frequency of the light waves should be appreciably slower than those received from a source here on earth. This would mean that these waves would be much longer and therefore redder in color. They would have been shifted toward the red end of the spectrum. Because the shift is caused by a gravitational field, it is called a "gravit-tional red shift." Astronomers have been able to measure such gravitational red shifts for several white dwarf stars. The measurements match the predicted amounts as computed from the equations of the theory of relativity.

That means that the frequency of the light waves from white dwarfs is slower than it is from sources here on earth. Since frequency is a measure of time itself, time passes more slowly on these stars than it does here on earth. Of course, if you were able to be on these stars, you would not be aware that time was passing more slowly. It would seem quite normal to you. Once again, we measure the passage of time by our own frame of reference. As we have seen before, time is not an absolute quantity, but depends upon where we are in the space-time continuum. It depends upon our frame of reference.

Einstein had started with the principle of equivalence and had redefined the concept of gravitation. His general theory of relativity really is a new theory of gravitation. He staked the validity of this theory on three predictions derived from his equations. He predicted the explanation for the extra 43 seconds of arc in Mercury's orbital rotation. He predicted the bending of light in the presence of a gravitational field. And he predicted the slowing down of time in a gravitational field. All three predictions were proved true. There has never been an experiment or test that has been able to refute any part of his theory.

The Saddle Universe

THE PLANET EARTH is one of nine planets that revolve around the sun. These planets and the sun are the major objects in our solar system. The sun is by far the largest of these objects, yet it is a very average-size star. It is one of the billions of stars that make up our galaxy, the Milky Way.

If we could shrink the size of our galaxy so that the earth was only one inch away from the sun, the next nearest star would still be 4 1/3 miles away from us! On that scale, our galaxy would be about 100,000 miles in diameter. Look at the photograph of the Andromeda galaxy. If the earth were one inch from the sun, the Andromeda galaxy would be two million miles away!

Note that some of the stars in the photograph of the Andromeda galaxy have much sharper images than the image of the galaxy itself. These stars are in our own galaxy and we are looking beyond them to the much more distant Andromeda galaxy.

Figure 41. If the earth were one inch from the sun, Andromeda galaxy would be two million miles away.

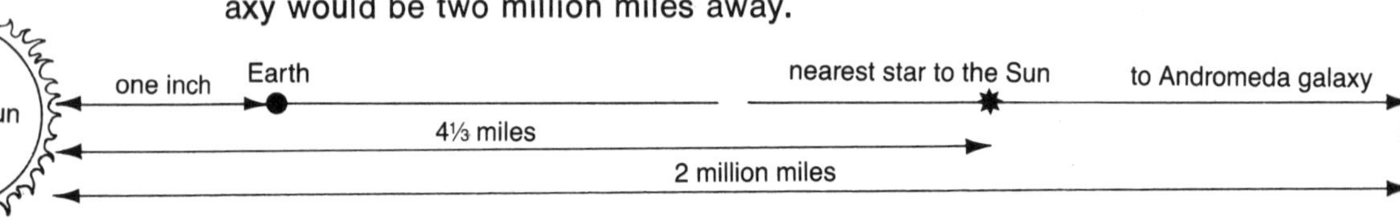

Dearborn Observatory photo

The Andromeda galaxy. Light from this vast star system takes more than 2 million years to reach us.

Because we are inside the Milky Way, we cannot see its shape or take a picture of it as was done for the Andromeda galaxy. That would be like trying to photograph your house while you were in your bedroom. However, by viewing other galaxies and learning more about our own, astronomers have determined that the Milky Way is very similar to many others. It is believed to look very much like the Andromeda galaxy.

In Figure 42 you can see where the sun is located within our galaxy. Note that it is not near the center but rather is far

Yerkes Observatory photo

A section of the Milky Way in the constellation Sagittarius. Each dot of light is an individual star.

off in the outer regions. It is in one of the "spiral arms" of the galaxy. There are several such arms curling around the center, or nucleus, of the galaxy. The Milky Way, like the Andromeda galaxy, is a "spiral galaxy." See if you can trace the arms in the picture of the Andromeda galaxy.

Special instruments are needed to trace the spiral arms in the Milky Way, but every clear night we can see where the plane of the galaxy is. When you look at the night sky, you will notice that some regions have more stars than others. But one area is

Figure 42.

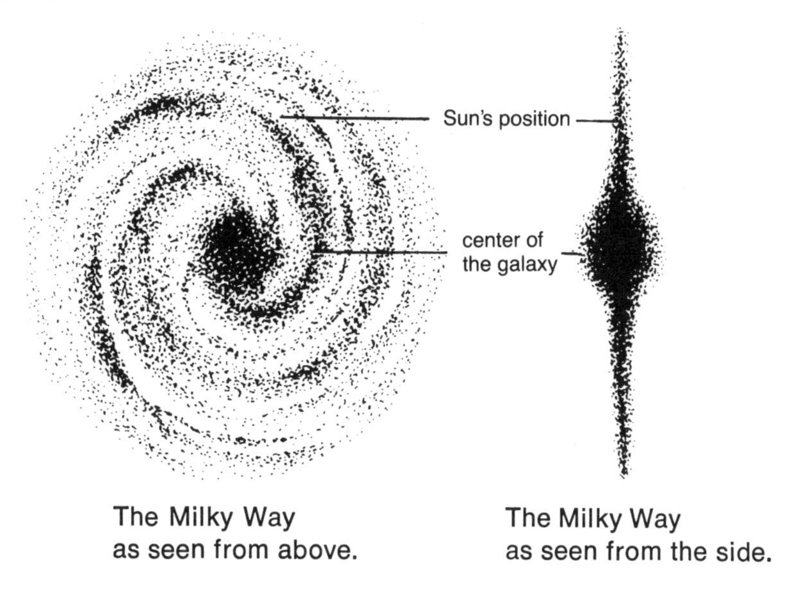

The Milky Way
as seen from above.

The Milky Way
as seen from the side.

so crowded with stars that you cannot separate them into individual stars. Instead you will see a faint, cloudlike band stretching across the entire sky. People long ago called this band the "pathway of the gods" or the "Milky Way," thus unknowingly naming our galaxy. They did not know that this band was actually made up of the light of thousands of stars. Only with a telescope or a good pair of binoculars can we see separate stars in this area of the sky.

When we look at the Milky Way in the sky, we are looking along the plane of our galaxy. It is the thickest part and therefore has the most stars. Because we are not at the very outskirts of the galaxy, we can see this cloudlike band in all directions. However, the densest region of stars is in the constellation Sagittarius, because that is the direction to the center of the galaxy.

None of this was known before the invention of the telescope

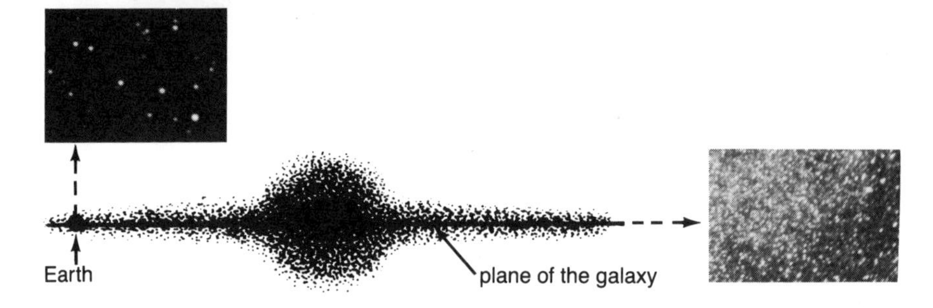

Figure 43. When we look at the Milky Way in the sky, we are looking along the plane of the galaxy, and therefore see many more stars than are visible elsewhere in the sky.

in the early seventeenth century. It was Galileo who first turned the telescope toward the sky and recorded what he saw there. Imagine his surprise upon seeing the cloudlike band become thousands of tiny points of light, each one an individual star! Galileo did not know the distances to these stars and therefore did not realize that this dense band of stars was the plane of our galaxy. But the invention of the telescope drastically changed the old concepts of the universe.

It was not until the eighteenth century that astronomers recognized this band of stars for what it was. But even then it was assumed that our sun was located at or near the center of this disk-shaped galaxy, which in turn was believed to be at the center of the universe. Actually, the universe of the eighteenth century consisted of only this galaxy. It was believed that this unique star system was like an island floating in an endless sea of space. All the matter in the universe was assumed to be located within this galaxy.

Although by then it was known that the stars move within the galaxy, the galaxy as a whole was thought not to change. It was considered a static universe both in size and in shape. Not until the 1920's was this picture of our universe finally proved to be false.

In 1924, the Andromeda galaxy was discovered to be located far outside of our own galaxy. Up until then, because its distance had not been determined, it had been considered a minor

Galileo's telescopes, now in a museum in Florence, Italy. Below the telescopes, in the center of the ivory frame, is one of the original lenses that Galileo used to discover the four major moons of Jupiter.

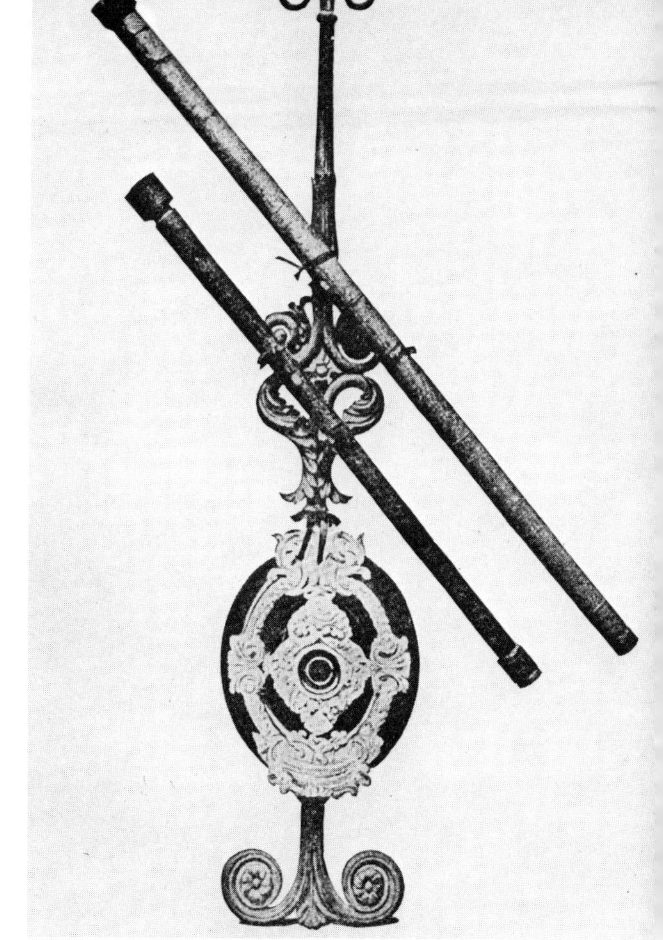

Yerkes Observatory photo

star system lying within the boundaries of the Milky Way. This was, of course, in keeping with the theory that there was nothing beyond our galaxy because that was considered to be the entire universe.* With time, other star systems were also found to be located outside the Milky Way and were recognized as separate and distinct galaxies. Today, it is estimated that there are at least a billion galaxies in the universe. Most of them are so far away that it takes their light millions of years

* In the late nineteenth century, two small satellite galaxies, the Large and Small Magellanic Clouds, were found to lie outside the Milky Way, but they were so close and so small that they were not considered truly independent island universes like our own.

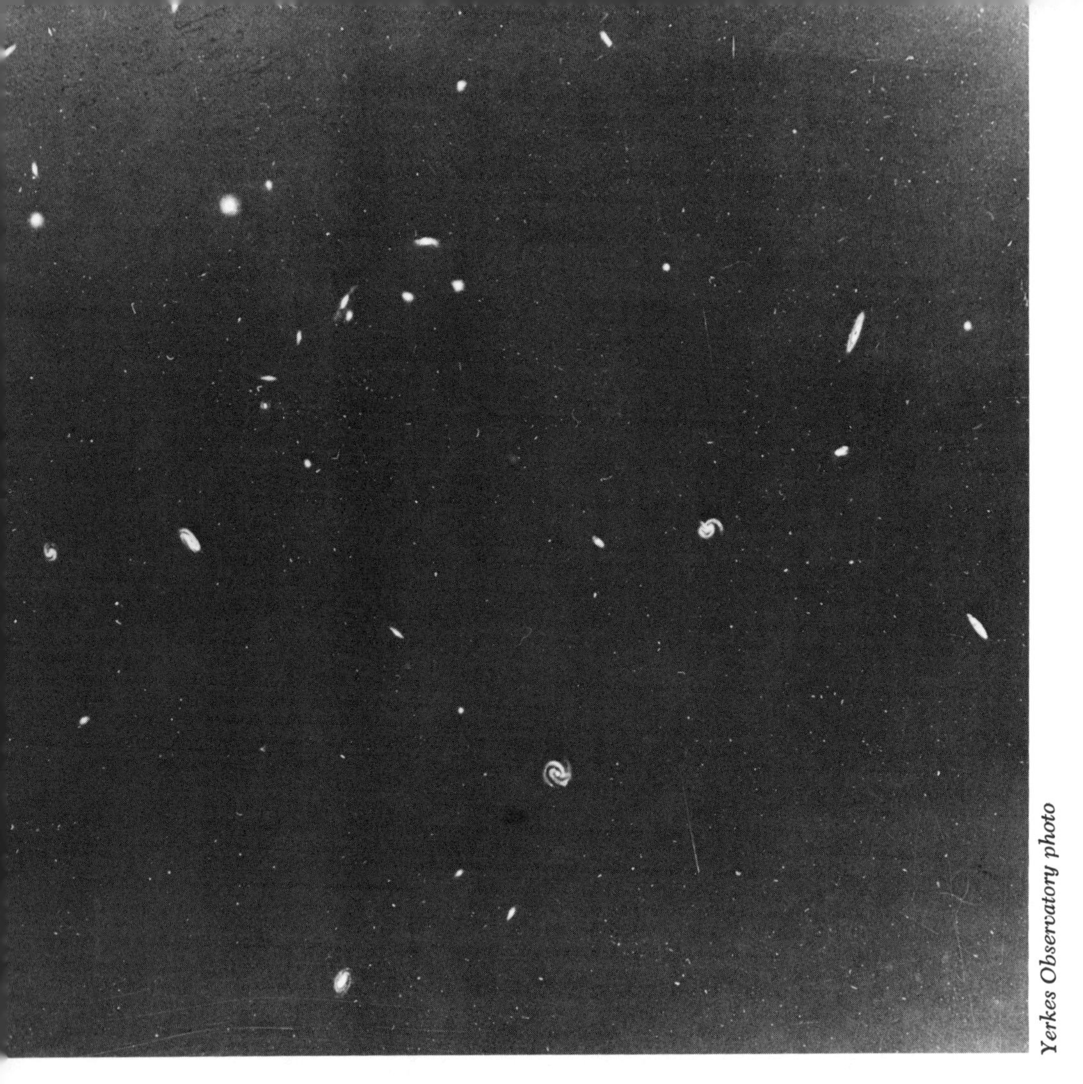

Yerkes Observatory photo

The cluster of galaxies in the constellation Virgo. Small as they may appear in the photograph, each blurry patch contains billions of stars. Although the Virgo cluster is one of the closest clusters of galaxies to us, it takes 78 million years for its light to reach us.

or more to reach us. Within the last sixty years, the size of the known universe has increased more than 10,000 times.

Albert Einstein presented his general theory of relativity in 1916, eight years before astronomers had proof that the Andromeda galaxy was located beyond the Milky Way. Considering the dominant scientific beliefs of his day, it is truly remarkable that he was able to present such a completely different picture of the world around us.

As we have seen, Newtonian theory was based upon Euclidean or flat (plane) geometry. Because the space-time in the solar system is curved very little, most observations agreed with this theory. However, long before Einstein challenged this theory it was known that Euclidean geometry could not be used on the surface of the earth.

We saw the effects of the curvature of the earth in Chapter Seven in our example of the airplane flying from Chicago to London. Euclidean geometry says that the shortest distance between two points is a straight line. On a curved surface, this is not true.

As another example, let us look at a simple geometrical shape, the triangle. According to Euclidean geometry, the angles of a triangle always add up to 180°. Draw a few triangles of different shapes and sizes and then measure their angles. You will find that the Euclidean theorem is true if you have used a flat sheet of paper.

Now let us consider a triangle on the surface of the earth. If it is a very small one, we will not be able to detect any difference between its angles and those that we drew on the piece of paper. But let us draw a large triangle whose base lies along the earth's equator. Each of its legs will follow lines of longitude, extending from the equator up to the north pole where they will meet. All of the lines of longitude intersect the equator at right angles, or 90°. (See Figure 44.) Therefore the two angles at the base of the triangle add up to 180°. The three angles of our triangle will add up to more than 180°. Euclidean geometry does not work on the earth's surface because it is not flat.

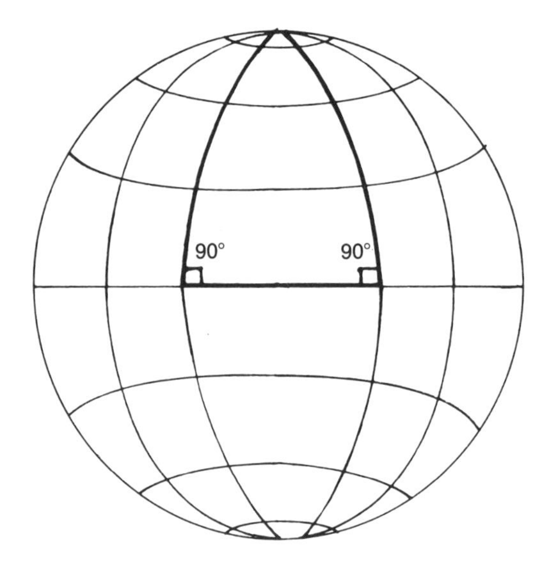

Figure 44. A large triangle on the earth's surface would have more than 180°.

Einstein pointed out our dependency upon Euclidean or flat geometry even though we know that its rules do not apply on our spherical earth. Why, he asked, do we assume that they apply to the universe as a whole? Is it not possible that an entirely different geometry must be used when discussing the size or shape of the universe? Every star, planet, moon or other massive body has a gravitational field around it which shapes its immediate space-time. Shouldn't all of this matter together have an effect upon the overall shape of the universe? What is the curvature of the space-time of the entire universe?

Before we discuss these questions and how they might be answered, we must first understand a very important astronomical phenomenon. Our universe is expanding; it is constantly growing bigger. When this fact was first discovered in 1929, it was difficult even for scientists to accept. Einstein had found earlier that his equations suggested such a phenomenon, but even he rejected it as being completely contrary to all available evidence of the early twentieth century.

Today there is no longer any argument about this dynamic nature of our universe. Proof of the expansion comes from astronomical observations of distant galaxies. Not only are all these galaxies moving away from us, but it has been found that the farther away a galaxy is, the faster it is receding. This does not mean that our galaxy, the Milky Way, is the center of the universe. The same recession would be noticed from every other galaxy regardless of its location. Let us use a thought experiment to clarify this.

Imagine an enormous classroom stretching as far as you can see. The desks are all in rows 2 feet apart. They start moving slowly away from each other so that during every ten-minute interval the space between the desks doubles. (See Figure 45.) If you were seated at Desk A, after ten minutes Desk B would be 4 feet from you. Desk C, which was only 4 feet from you originally, would now be 8 feet away. And Desk D, which was 6 feet away, would now be 12 feet away. B has only moved 2 feet in ten minutes whereas C has moved 4 feet and D has moved 6 feet. Obviously D, in order to move three times the distance that B moved in the same period of time, has had to have a velocity three times faster than B's.

The person in Desk D, observing this same expansion of the space between the desks, would see your desk move away from his three times faster than C's desk. No one could say that his desk was the center one. Each would see the more distant desks moving away faster than the closer ones. Note also that the desks themselves did not "expand," only the space between them.

You can make a simple model of such an expansion with a toy balloon and some cotton balls. Glue the cotton balls all over the partially inflated balloon. Now finish blowing up the balloon. The space between the cotton balls will increase. If you measure this space before and after the final inflation of the balloon, you can prove that the tufts farthest away from each other increase their distance the most.

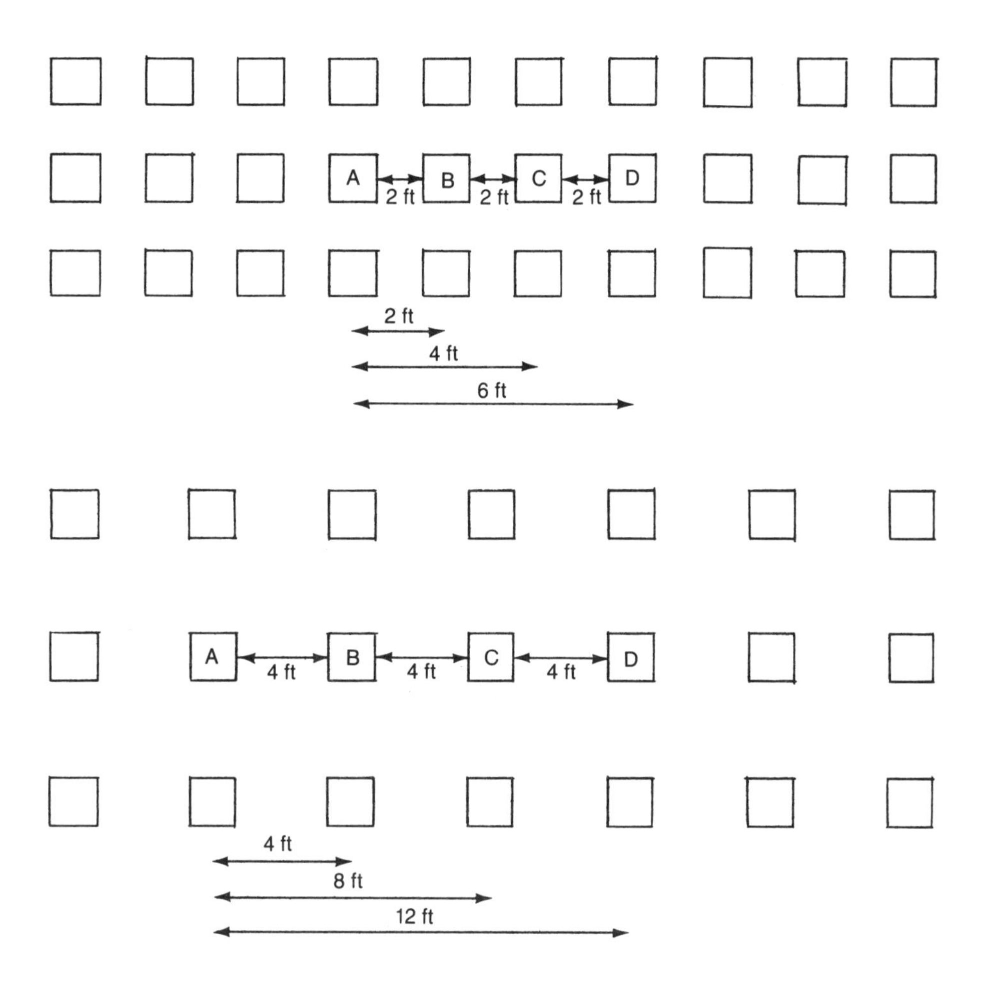

Figure 45. Thought experiment: the expanding classroom. Classroom desks are 2 feet apart. Ten minutes later, the desks are 4 feet apart.

The desks or the tufts of cotton represent the galaxies. The space between them is the space-time continuum. It is the space-time that is expanding, not the matter itself. From our observations of the matter (the stars and galaxies) we can determine how far into the universe we can see. This is the extent of the "observable universe," but it is not necessarily the entire universe. Very distant galaxies are known to be receding from us at velocities approaching the speed of light. Those closer to us are moving away much more slowly. Was there a time when everything was back together? When did this expansion begin?

Calculations based upon the velocities of these distant galaxies indicate that about 15 to 18 billion years ago our universe was a single chaotic mass of matter and energy. This extremely compact mass is believed to have exploded, starting the expansion outward. This cosmological theory, which is named after that initial explosion, is called the "Big Bang" theory. It is the one accepted by most astronomers today. Further proof of its accuracy came in 1965 when radiation left over from the Big Bang was actually detected. Scientists had predicted earlier that such radiation was still coursing through the universe, though much weaker than in its original form.

If the universe started with a Big Bang and has been expanding ever since, the next question is whether it will keep on expanding forever. Or will it eventually slow down and start to contract back again into an infinitely compact ball of matter and energy? If it did become a primeval mass at some time in the very distant future, the assumption is that it would then explode once more and repeat the expansion-contraction cycle again and again. This is called the "Oscillating Universe" theory.

The path the universe will follow (continued expansion or eventual contraction) depends upon how much matter there is in the universe. As we have seen, the presence of matter creates a gravitational field which affects the curvature of the space-time continuum. Up until now we have been concentrating upon small regions of this space-time to show how matter affected it. Just as each object's gravitational field curves the space-time in its vicinity, on a much bigger scale the total

Yerkes Observatory photo

The 40-inch refracting telescope at Yerkes Observatory, Williams Bay, Wisconsin. The primary lens of this telescope has a diameter of 40 inches. That is about 40 times larger than Galileo's first telescope lens.

amount of matter in the universe curves the overall space-time continuum. We therefore know that our universe cannot be flat; it must have some curvature to it.

If there is enough matter in the universe gravitationally to slow down the expansion and cause the universe to contract again, then the overall curvature of the space-time continuum is "positive." That is, mathematically speaking, it will curve back upon itself like a ball. We call such a universe "closed." This is the kind of universe in which theoretically you could keep traveling in one direction and ultimately arrive back at your starting point.

If the universe does not have the required amount of matter necessary for it to "close" itself, it will not be able to stop or

Figure 46.

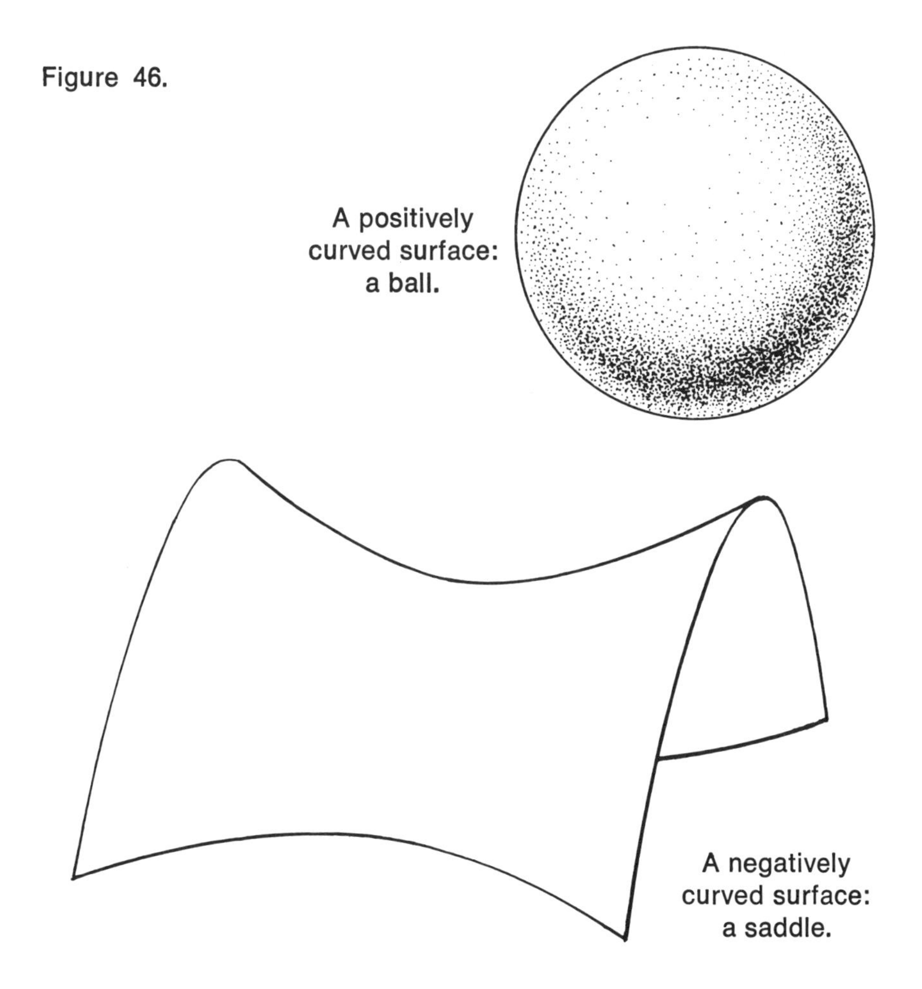

to slow down the expansion. It will keep expanding into infinity in both space and time. The curvature of the space-time continuum in such a universe is, in mathematical terms, "negative." It is curved like a saddle. Mathematically we call such a curve a "hyperbola." Such a universe is "open" and therefore a space traveler would never return to his original point if he kept going in the same direction.

Do not be disappointed if you cannot visualize such universes. Their descriptions are derived from mathematical equations and are the simplest way that scientists and mathematicians have to explain what they are looking for. They have been trying to detect a specific amount of matter in the universe which they have calculated will cause the universal expansion to slow down enough to cause it eventually to reverse itself. Besides the amount of matter, there are other clues that will indicate whether such a slowing down is occurring.

Thus far, however, all the evidence points to an "open" universe. The universe is not slowing down its expansion enough to cause it eventually to begin to contract. There is not enough matter in the universe to stop the expansion gravitationally, and therefore we must conclude that the universe will expand forever.

A New Language

IT MUST HAVE been very difficult for the people of the sixteenth and seventeenth centuries to accept the facts that the earth is spherical and that it revolves about the sun. It probably was equally difficult for those living in the early twentieth century to believe that the universe was not just the Milky Way but a billion galaxies or more spread out over an unimaginable expanse.

These galaxies are rushing away from us, with those farthest away moving the fastest. But we are not the central point. There is no center of the universe, just as there is no "center" on the surface of the earth. Not only is our enormous universe expanding, but it will continue to expand forever. There is not enough matter in the universe to slow up this expansion gravitationally and eventually pull everything back together again.

Can we ever accept such ideas, which go beyond our world of experience and which contradict our sense perceptions? Yes, we will adjust to these new ideas just as people centuries ago adjusted to the fact that the earth was round and that it revolved around the sun. Those discoveries also are contrary to what our senses tell us.

Our language still reflects the earlier ideas. For example, we still speak of sunrise and sunset even though we know that it is not the motion of the sun that causes these events. We see the sun move down to the horizon and disappear below it. Our

NASA photograph taken by Apollo 11 astronauts

Half-earth, as seen from the moon. Only 25 years ago such a photograph could only be dreamed about. What new vistas will be opened up 25 or 200 years from now?

senses tell us that the sun is moving. We do not feel the earth turning. We would require some sophisticated equipment to prove that it does, in fact, turn on its axis once every twenty-four hours.

When we flick on a light switch, our room seems to be immediately filled with light. Our senses tell us that light takes no time at all to travel. That is because our powers of observation are not sufficiently sensitive to detect the minute amount of time needed for the light to cross the room. We need special instruments to measure the velocity of light.

On a star-studded night, the sky appears as an inverted bowl covered with brilliantly shining points of light. People long ago believed that this "celestial sphere" was real. It was supposed to be made of some sort of hard material in which the stars were embedded. It turned around the earth so that the stars rose and then set each night. It is not hard to imagine such a sphere. We have no depth perception when we look at the sky, even with a telescope. All the stars do appear to be at the same distance. Once again we cannot trust what our senses alone tell us. Only with telescopes and measuring instruments can we determine the true distances of the stars. What we see and what really is are not always the same.

When Albert Einstein first presented his theory of relativity, he did not know the true extent of the universe. He did not know that it was expanding. But he did realize that in order to know the true nature of this universe, we cannot rely solely upon what our senses tell us.

We are, in a way, imprisoned by our limited powers of observation here on this earth. We cannot visualize billions of galaxies or a universe that will expand forever. Nor can we visualize the structure of the atom or the minuteness of the tiniest subatomic particles. If you find that contemplation of

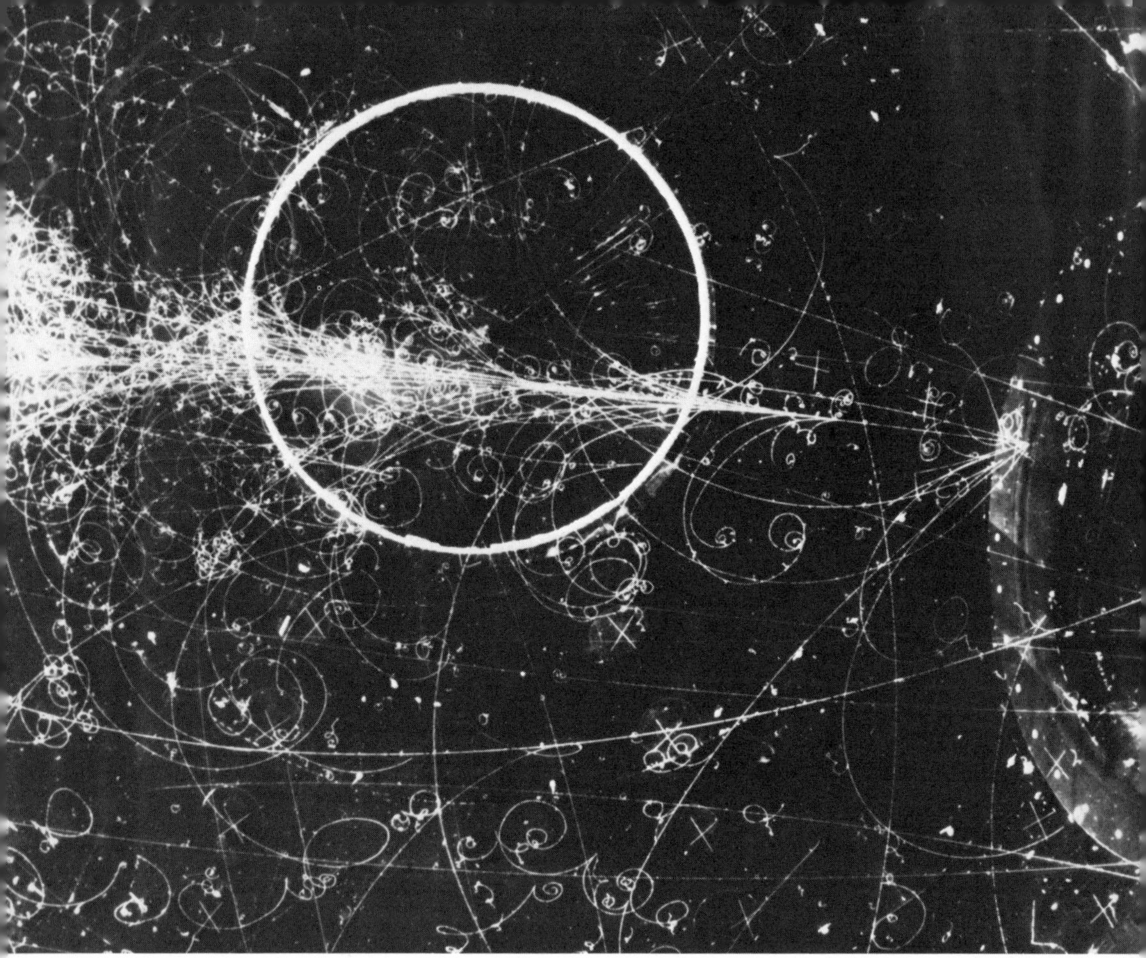

Yerkes Observatory photo

The tracks of subatomic particles. A stream of particles emerges from a proton that has been bombarded by a very high-energy particle. The particle tracks are actually a series of bubbles which form in the very hot hydrogen gas inside the "bubble chamber."

the vast cosmos makes you feel very insignificant, consider this: The largest object in the universe is as much bigger than a human as the tiniest subatomic particle is smaller. Perhaps that is why the prime mysteries of nature lie in these two extremes of reality. Perhaps that is why we cannot describe either in ordinary language. The scientist must use mathematical relalationships—equations—to describe and to study these areas.

The theory of relativity consists mainly of such equations. They mathematically describe the universe, not as we see it or think it should be, but as it really is. How do we know that these equations are correct? They have been proved true in many experiments and tests. They have explained phenomena which other theories couldn't. And they have predicted phenomena which other theories never even mentioned.

The theory of relativity is not the end of our story, but rather the beginning of a much more important one. It is a new alphabet from which a new language will develop. The adventure of exploring new realms awaits future scientists. There are many uncharted fields to challenge them. Perhaps one of these scientists will be you!

Glossary

ACCELERATION: the rate of change in velocity, either speeding up, slowing down, or changing direction.

ALTITUDE: height; in aviation, it is usually the height above sea level.

ANDROMEDA GALAXY: a large spiral galaxy similar to the Milky Way.

APHELION: the point in a planet's orbit at which it is farthest from the sun.

ASTRONAUT: a person who travels in a spacecraft beyond the earth's atmosphere.

ATOM: the smallest particle of an element which still keeps the characteristics of that element.

ATOMIC CLOCK: a timekeeping device regulated by the vibrations of atoms or molecules.

BIG BANG THEORY: the cosmological theory that states that the universe had its origin in the violent explosion of a primeval mass.

BLACK HOLE: an extremely compacted astronomical object whose gravitational field is powerful enough to curve space-time so that radiation in that region cannot escape.

BLUE SHIFT: a decrease in the wavelength of electromagnetic radiation.

"CELESTIAL SPHERE": the apparent sphere of the sky.

CHARGED PARTICLE: a subatomic particle that has either a negative or positive electric charge.

COMET: a loose collection of dust, gas, and particles of ice which revolves around the sun, usually in an elongated orbit.

CONTINUUM: a continuous series of parts passing into one another without any division or boundary.

COORDINATES: measurements that are used to position an object in a continuum.

CORONA: the outermost atmosphere of the sun; visible only during a total solar eclipse.

COSMIC RAYS: rapidly moving atomic nuclei (mostly protons) which fall upon the earth from outer space.

COSMOLOGY: the study of the origin and evolution of the universe.

COSMOS: the entire universe.

ELECTROMAGNETIC RADIATION: all forms of radiation energy from gamma rays through the spectrum of light to the longest radio waves.

ELECTROMAGNETIC SPECTRUM: the range of electromagnetic radiation arranged in order of increasing wavelength.

ELECTRON: a negatively charged subatomic particle normally revolving around the nucleus of an atom.

ELEMENT: a substance consisting of atoms which are all the same.

ENERGY: the ability to do work.

"ETHER": a "substance" formerly thought to fill all the space in the universe and to carry light waves.

EUCLIDEAN GEOMETRY: plane geometry; valid in flat space-time.

EVENT: a point on a world line in four-dimensional space-time.

FRAME OF REFERENCE: a coordinate system from which an individual observes and measures the world around him.

FREQUENCY (of electromagnetic waves): in astronomy and physics, the number of electromagnetic waves passing a given point in a given period of time.

GALAXY: a vast system of stars such as our own galaxy, the Milky Way.

GAMMA RAYS: a form of electromagnetic radiation with the smallest wavelengths and the highest frequency.

GENERAL THEORY: that part of Einstein's theory of relativity that deals with non-uniform motion and leads to a theory of gravitation that explains it in terms of the geometry of space-time.

GEODESIC: the shortest distance between two points in any given geometry; the path of a body in space-time.

GRAVITATION (Newtonian): the attractive force exhibited between any two material particles; gravity.

GRAVITATIONAL FIELD (Newtonian): the region around any body which exerts an attractive force on another body.

GRAVITATIONAL FIELD (Einsteinian): the region around a body in which the space-time continuum is warped.

GRAVITATIONAL RED SHIFT: the red shift caused by a strong gravitational field; sometimes called the "Einstein shift."

HELIUM: the second lightest and second most abundant element in the universe; a gas.

HYDROGEN: the lightest and most abundant element in the universe; usually found in a gaseous form.

HYPOTHESIS: a tentative theory which is proposed to explain certain phenomena or observed facts; further tests and verifications are necessary before it becomes an accepted theory.

INTERVAL: the distance in space-time between two events.

JUPITER: the fifth planet from the sun; the largest and most massive planet in the solar system.

LATITUDE: a north-south coordinate on the surface of the earth.

LAW OF UNIVERSAL GRAVITATION: Newton's mathematical statement or formula for the attractive force between two material objects.

LIGHT: electromagnetic radiation that is visible to the eye.

LONGITUDE: an east-west coordinate on the surface of the earth.

MAGNETIC FIELD: the region of space near a magnetized object in which a magnetic force can be detected.

MAJOR AXIS: the longest dimension across an ellipse.

MASS: a measure of the total amount of matter in an object.

MERCURY: the nearest planet to the sun; the smallest planet in the solar system, with the exception of Pluto.

MESON: a subatomic particle with a mass between that of a proton and an electron.

MILKY WAY: our galaxy; also the faint ragged band of light that cuts across the night sky.

MINOR AXIS: the shortest dimension of an ellipse passing through the central point.

MOLECULE: two or more atoms bound together.

MUON: a "mu meson"; a subatomic particle with a mass between that of a proton and an electron.

NEUTRON: a subatomic particle with no charge and with mass about equal to that of a proton; one of the two main particles of the atomic nucleus.

NUCLEAR: pertaining to the nucleus of the atom.

NUCLEUS (of atom): the heaviest part of an atom; its central part, composed of protons and neutrons; plural is "nuclei."

NUCLEUS (of galaxy): central portion of a galaxy; plural is "nuclei."

OBSERVABLE UNIVERSE: that part of the universe which scientists can detect.

ORBIT: the actual path in space of a celestial object as it revolves about another body in space.

OSCILLATING UNIVERSE THEORY: a cosmological theory which states that the universe alternately expands and contracts.

PERIHELION: the point in a planet's orbit at which it is nearest the sun.

PERIOD: a time interval; the time required for a return to the same position or situation, such as the time for one complete revolution around the sun.

PERIOD OF REVOLUTION: the time it takes one body to orbit completely around another body.

PERIOD OF TOTALITY: (see *totality*)

PERTURBATION: a small disturbance in the motion of a body caused by the gravitational attraction of another object.

PRINCIPLE OF EQUIVALENCE: a principle of general relativity that states that the effects of acceleration and gravitation cannot be distinguished; they are the same.

PROTON: a heavy, positively charged subatomic particle; one of the two main particles of the atomic nucleus.

RADIATION: all forms of electromagnetic energy.

RED SHIFT: an increase in the wavelength of electromagnetic radiation.

RELATIVITY: (see *general theory* and *special theory*)

REVOLUTION: the motion of one celestial body around another.

ROTATION: the turning of a body about its own axis.

SOLAR SYSTEM: the sun, the planets and their moons, the minor planets (asteroids), comets, and other objects revolving around the sun.

SPACE-TIME: a four-dimensional continuum in which three dimensions are spatial and one is temporal; also called the space-time continuum.

SPECIAL THEORY: that part of the theory of relativity which deals with uniform motion; it describes how the measurement of physical phenomena such as time or mass depends upon the relative velocity of the observer and the object being observed.

SPECTRUM: the array of wavelengths or color when electromagnetic radiation is spread out into the colors of the rainbow.

SPIRAL GALAXY: a galaxy which is pinwheel-shaped with "arms" that spiral away from the nucleus.

SPUTNIK: the name given to the first Soviet artificial satellite; its launching was the beginning of the space age.

SUBATOMIC PARTICLES: particles of matter which are smaller than and form a part of an atom; sometimes called "elementary particles."

SYNCHROTRON: a particle accelerator.

SYNCHROTRON RADIATION: electromagnetic radiation from charged particles moving near the velocity of light in a magnetic field.

THEORY: a set of hypotheses that have been well verified.

THOUGHT EXPERIMENT: an imaginary test situation developed in order to reach solutions to specific problems.

TIME DILATION: the phenomenon whereby the clocks and other time processes of a moving object appear to run more slowly as measured by a stationary observer.

TOTAL SOLAR ECLIPSE: an eclipse of the sun in which its entire disk is hidden by the moon.

TOTALITY: the period in a total eclipse of the sun during which the bright surface of the sun is totally obscured from view on the earth by the moon.

UNIVERSE: all matter and energy in existence and the space it occupies; the cosmos.

VENUS: the second planet from the sun.

WAVELENGTH: the distance between successive crests in a series of waves.

WEIGHT: a measure of the earth's (or other massive body's) gravitational force upon a given mass.

WHITE DWARF: a star in its last stages of evolution that has used up all or most of its nuclear fuel and has collapsed into a very small size.

WORLD LINE: the path of an object in space-time.

Index

Italics indicate photograph